Harvard
Business
Review

ON

DOING BUSINESS IN CHINA

D0062475

THE HARVARD BUSINESS REVIEW PAPERBACK SERIES

The series is designed to bring today's managers and professionals the fundamental information they need to stay competitive in a fast-moving world. From the preeminent thinkers whose work has defined an entire field to the rising stars who will redefine the way we think about business, here are the leading minds and landmark ideas that have established the *Harvard Business Review* as required reading for ambitious businesspeople in organizations around the globe.

Other books in the series:

Harvard Business Review Interviews with CEOs

Harvard Business Review on Advances in Strategy

Harvard Business Review on Becoming a High Performance Manager

Harvard Business Review on Brand Management

Harvard Business Review on Breakthrough Leadership

Harvard Business Review on Breakthrough Thinking

Harvard Business Review on Building Personal and Organizational Resilience

Harvard Business Review on Business and the Environment

Harvard Business Review on the Business Value of IT

Harvard Business Review on Change

Harvard Business Review on Compensation

Harvard Business Review on Corporate Ethics

Harvard Business Review on Corporate Governance

Harvard Business Review on Corporate Responsibility

Harvard Business Review on Corporate Strategy

Harvard Business Review on Crisis Management

Harvard Business Review on Culture and Change

Harvard Business Review on Customer Relationship Management

Harvard Business Review on Decision Making

Other books in the series (continued):

Harvard Business Review on Developing Leaders

Harvard Business Review on Effective Communication

Harvard Business Review on Entrepreneurship

Harvard Business Review on Finding and Keeping the Best People

Harvard Business Review on Innovation

Harvard Business Review on the Innovative Enterprise

Harvard Business Review on Knowledge Management

Harvard Business Review on Leadership

Harvard Business Review on Leadership at the Top

Harvard Business Review on Leadership in a Changed World

Harvard Business Review on Leading in Turbulent Times

Harvard Business Review on Managing Diversity

Harvard Business Review on Managing High-Tech Industries

Harvard Business Review on Managing People

Harvard Business Review on Managing Uncertainty

Harvard Business Review on Managing the Value Chain

Harvard Business Review on Managing Your Career

Harvard Business Review on Marketing

Harvard Business Review on Measuring Corporate Performance

Harvard Business Review on Mergers and Acquisitions

Harvard Business Review on Motivating People

Harvard Business Review on Negotiation and Conflict Resolution

Harvard Business Review on Nonprofits

Harvard Business Review on Organizational Learning

Harvard Business Review on Strategic Alliances

Harvard Business Review on Strategies for Growth

Harvard Business Review on Teams That Succeed

Harvard Business Review on Turnarounds

Harvard Business Review on Work and Life Balance

Harvard
Business
Review

ON

DOING BUSINESS IN CHINA

A HARVARD BUSINESS REVIEW PAPERBACK

Copyright 2004
Harvard Business School Publishing Corporation
All rights reserved
Printed in the United States of America
08 07 06 05   5 4 3

No part of this publication may be reproduced, stored in or introduced
into a retrieval system, or transmitted, in any form, or by any means
(electronic, mechanical, photocopying, recording, or otherwise),
without the prior permission of the publisher. Requests for permission
should be directed to permissions@hbsp.harvard.edu, or mailed to
Permissions, Harvard Business School Publishing, 60 Harvard Way,
Boston, Massachusetts 02163.

The *Harvard Business Review* articles in this collection are available as
individual reprints. Discounts apply to quantity purchases. For information and ordering, please contact Customer Service, Harvard Business
School Publishing, Boston, MA 02163. Telephone: (617) 783-7500 or
(800) 988-0886, 8 A.M. to 6 P.M. Eastern Time, Monday through Friday.
Fax: (617) 783-7555, 24 hours a day. E-mail: custserv@hbsp.harvard.edu

Library of Congress Cataloging-in-Publication Data
Harvard business review on doing business in China.
        p.   cm. — (The Harvard business review paperback series)
    Includes index.
    ISBN 1-59139-638-7
    1. International business enterprises—China. 2. Business enter-
prises, Foreign—China. 3. Investments, Foreign—China. 4. China—
Commerce. 5. China—Commercial policy. I. Harvard business
review. II. Series.
HD9210.H37 2004

                                                    2004016128
                                                          CIP

*The paper used in this publication meets the minimum requirements of
the American National Standard for Information Sciences—Perma-
nence of Paper for Printed Library Materials, ANSI Z39.48–1992.*

Contents

Harvard Business Review

ON

DOING BUSINESS IN CHINA

The Great Transition

KENNETH LIEBERTHAL AND

GEOFFREY LIEBERTHAL

Executive Summary

AS CHINA'S ECONOMY GROWS and opens further,
the opportunity it presents to multinationals is changing.
Foreign companies are moving to country development
and new strategic choices. Now, foreign firms can actually go after the Chinese domestic market, and it's worth
going after. Improvements in China's infrastructure, workforce, and regulatory environment are making it possible
for companies to lower their costs to reap new competitive advantages.

Multifaceted and often-shifting risks accompany this
shifting opportunity. The reforms required for admission
into the WTO will be politically difficult for China to
implement, and its progress will be slowed by the
scarcity of resources for the country's shaky banking system, the inadequacy of the social safety net, environmental problems, and local governments' cash shortage.

1

China's breathtaking 9% average annual GDP growth rests on an unsteady foundation of overcapitalized state-owned enterprises, which have oversupplied many markets, and fiercely protectionist regional government officials pursuing growth-at-almost-all-costs policies. Frequent changes in regulations, bureaucracies, and reporting relationships will continue to make planning difficult, and, as the SARS epidemic demonstrated, there is always the potential for serious disruptions.

But for at least the next ten years, multinationals should be the biggest winners in China. To reap the benefits, a multinational must properly nest its effort into its overall organization, show "one face to China" at the national level but also tailor local strategies, be wary of joint ventures, and mitigate risk, in particular the theft of intellectual property. China is a major opportunity for companies that forthrightly face its complexities. It will remain largely inscrutable—and unprofitable—for the rest.

CHINA IS ATTRACTING ENORMOUS attention for very good reason. The reason is not just that China is big or that its economy is the only one that's been able to sustain rapid growth over the last three years. It's that China is now profoundly affecting the competitive capabilities of all multinational corporations. Companies throughout the world are affected by the impact of low-cost Chinese manufacturing on worldwide pricing, for instance, whether or not they have operations there or engage in direct trade.

Beneath the surface of China's enormous accomplishments is a complicated story: The country's astonishing growth and exploding domestic market promise huge opportunities. But that growth also masks systemic weaknesses. China's comparative manufacturing advantage makes it an alluring platform from which to export to the rest of the world. But that platform sits in a fast-changing and high-risk operating environment that has frustrated many firms' quests for profits.

When China first timorously opened its economy to foreign investment in 1979, the rules tightly restricted the locations, sectors, and types of participation open to foreigners. As those rules gradually relaxed over the ensuing decades, the fortunes of international firms improved incrementally. But the real sea change in China's importance has occurred only in the past few years, as China has begun to implement its World Trade Organization accession obligations, and the country has stood out so sharply as the only rapidly growing major economy in the world. The opportunities, the risks, and the importance of understanding how to fit China into a corporate competitive strategy are entering a new stage—more dynamic, complex, and consequential for multinationals' success than ever before. Unraveling the complexities of those opportunities and risks can make the difference between major opportunity and major disappointment.

An Amazing Record

China's overall record since reforms began in 1979 is dazzling, and its performance is in many ways improving. Annual real GDP has grown about 9% a year, on average, since 1978—an aggregate increase of some 700%. Foreign trade growth has averaged nearly 15% over the same period, or more than 2,700% in aggregate. Foreign direct investment has flooded into the country, especially throughout the past decade. In 2002, China became the first country since the 1980s to attract more FDI in a year than the United States (bringing in $53.2 billion while $52.7 billion flowed into the States). In the first quarter of 2003, a billion dollars a month in foreign capital poured into the Pearl River Delta near Hong Kong, where integrated clusters of suppliers and assemblers are becoming an awesomely efficient manufacturing base for exports of everything from circuit boards to machinery to shoes to tools. Led by businesses there, China has rapidly moved to take its place among the world's largest trading nations. (See the exhibit "Unflagging Growth.") The country has developed a powerful combination—a disciplined, low-cost labor force; a large cadre of technical personnel; tax and other incentives to attract investment; and infrastructure sufficient to support efficient manufacturing operations and exports.

Like its export base, China's home market is growing strongly—in several segments, spectacularly. Four to six million new cell phone subscribers are signing up every month, for instance. Computer use is spreading more rapidly than in any other country. The automotive market is surging, making China the one place in the coming decade where carmakers can compete for a pie that is growing rather than fight over one that is not. In the early 1990s, almost all retail outlets in China were small shops and wet markets. Now, at least in major cities, hypermarkets are common. Firms such as Carrefour and Wal-Mart are rapidly expanding their investments to compete for this growing Chinese market.

Long-term trends in China, moreover, promise continued growth. The country has vastly improved its elite educational institutions and is quickly expanding its pool of technical talent. China graduated a million technicians and engineers in 2001. That figure leapt to 2 million in 2003 and will go still higher in 2004. And the quality of engineering training has improved to the extent that fewer Chinese are now going to the United States for engineering degrees because they can obtain excellent educations more cheaply at home. Japanese firms have long kept their China investments very limited because of concerns about the quality of the labor force. But since 2000, Japanese firms have not only been making increasingly high-end investments in China but also shifting investment resources there from Southeast Asia.

Ideologically, the country has shifted dramatically. Where once the Communist Party shut down China's universities and sent professors to be "reeducated"

Unflagging Growth

If future growth resembles that of the last five years, China's economy will be nearly the size of Germany's by 2008.

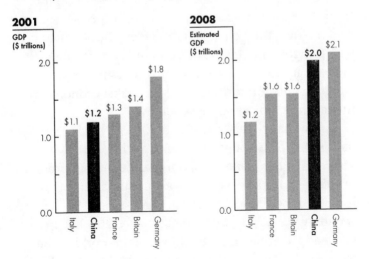

Note: Estimated 2008 GDP calculated by applying 1998–2002 GDP CAGR to 2001 GDP figure and compounding annually to 2008; China growth rate based on 1997–2001 GDP CAGR.

Source: World Bank for 2001 GDP figures; Economist.com country fact sheets for GDP CAGRs.

among the peasantry, now it welcomes professionals and entrepreneurs as part of the party's political base and foresees development of the private manufacturing and service sectors as the key job generators in the coming years.

To cope with the decline in demand brought on by the 1997 Asian financial crisis, China made massive infrastructure investments, including a vast expansion of the rail, highway, telecom, and water management systems. These investments have improved connections among what used to be largely separate domestic markets.

The regulatory environment is also moving in the right direction, becoming more transparent. As China implements its WTO commitments, more opportunities are opening up to foreign firms, which are increasingly being placed on an equal footing with indigenous companies. By 2006, for example, foreign financial service firms will be permitted to provide a full array of banking services. That should begin to nudge access to capital from state-owned enterprises toward the private sector. And the structural changes adopted by the National People's Congress in March 2003 portend additional progress in shifting the role of government from the planning and administration of a socialist economy to the regulation of a market economy.

These changes are massive, but, surprisingly, they have unfolded without the type of major political breakdown—like the Tiananmen uprising and its suppression in 1989—that made earlier investors rue the day they leapt into the Chinese market. What's more, the Chinese economy has not only grown but moved steadily up the value-added scale. In 1990, China led the world in the production of only cotton textiles and televisions. By 2002, it had added refrigerators, cameras, motorbikes, desktop PCs, DVD players, bicycles, cigarette lighters, and cellular phones to this list. China, in sum, is rapidly becoming the manufacturing center of Asia.

Beijing expects to maintain its low-cost labor advantage: Migration from the interior is keeping low-end labor rates—even along the booming coast—very competitive. At the same time, China believes it can develop niche capabilities in high-end areas such as computer hardware and biotechnology (where its regulatory environment gives it inherent advantages over Western countries). Moreover, the reformers in the government plan to use the WTO entry requirements to force the domestic reforms that they believe will make Chinese firms competitive internationally in the coming decades. So, in a remarkably wide range of sectors, multinationals must now think seriously about the ways their own China plays and those of their current and potential competitors can affect their wider future global opportunities.

A Golden Opportunity for Multinationals

For the next ten years, and probably considerably longer, multinationals (if not all of their employees) should be the biggest winners, as China's economy becomes increasingly open. During this period, few indigenous manufacturing and service-sector firms will be able to compete successfully outside the country on any basis other than cheap labor. (By "indigenous," we mean Chinese firms that have not attracted investments from any foreign companies and are not producing anything under foreign license.) There are, of course, some exceptions. A handful of Chinese companies are already strong competitors in global markets: Haier in white goods, Konka in TVs, Galanz in microwave ovens, and Huawei in telecommunications, for instance. And cheap labor matters, of course, even in sophisticated industries such as automobile assembly and telecom equipment. To date, manufacturers in Hong Kong and Taiwan have proven particularly adept at leveraging inexpensive mainland Chinese workers for international competitive advantage.

Weak management is the major constraint on the competitiveness of Chinese companies. Despite two decades of joint ventures and enormous investments in training, Chinese managers continue to fail in the critical tasks of systems integration and optimization. The problem is fundamental, embedded in the economic system itself. The dominance of state-owned enterprises in major manufacturing and service sectors, together with extensive state intervention throughout the economy, has sustained the premium on good political skills over modern management capabilities. The consequences are felt all the way down corporate hierarchies. Chinese firms generally view middle managers merely as information links and discipline enforcers rather than as partners in the search for new ideas and improved processes. On balance, the stovepiped authority structures and emphasis on obedience to higher authorities make Chinese managers good at carrying out discrete tasks but poor at optimizing all the processes in a value chain. This subtle deficiency is reflected in the absence of a Chinese term for the very concept of "trade-off."

In the military arena, for example, major weapon systems increasingly require the integration of complex subsystems. But despite large investments, the country's military-industrial complex has failed so completely to produce advanced integrated weapon systems that China has become highly reliant on Russian and Israeli imports.

China's management shortcomings were on display in 2003 during the outbreak of Severe Acute Respiratory Syndrome (SARS). Despite extensive investments in gene mapping and genomics in an effort to create a world-class biotechnology industry, the leading Chinese research institutes fell significantly behind their foreign counterparts in understanding the virus. The Chinese media, based on interviews at the research institutes, blame this primarily on the failure of the institutes to cooperate, as each waited for specific orders from higher government levels before turning to SARS research. This response reflected a management conditioned to operate according to preset plans and to avoid taking initiative at lower levels.

To be sure, Chinese managers and workers have become efficient at implementing decisions made by others. And few are better than the Chinese at small-scale entrepreneurship. But it will take decades to overcome the ingrained systemic weaknesses that prevent them from designing efficient enterprises, fostering innovation, allowing flexibility at middle management levels, and finding optimal trade-offs along various points in the value chain. In this respect, the situation in China differs totally from the competitive challenge to Western companies that Japan presented a quarter-century ago. Japan's secret sauce was management; but that is China's weakness. Domestic system reforms will over the long run produce internationally competitive indigenous Chinese firms. But, paradoxically, for the time being, the better and more efficient China's economy becomes, the more the advantages will accrue to multinational corporations.

China's domestic market is certainly one new opportunity. Until recently, China used tariff and especially nontariff barriers such as secret domestic quotas on imports and excessive inspection requirements to shield domestic producers from international competition, and it required foreign investors to form joint ventures to play at all. Many companies invested in China hoping to gain access to the domestic market but found instead that the government insisted they channel much of their production into exports. The results are clear. In every year save one since 1979, the country has run a trade surplus, with firms that foreign companies have invested in providing a steadily increasing proportion of the items exported. Over three-quarters of China's electronics exports come from enterprises invested in by foreign (including Hong Kong, Macao, and Taiwan) firms, for instance, and more than half of all exports are from the processing trade, made up of export products that have been assembled and packaged in China from imported components. The vast majority of such processing operations are owned or invested in by foreigners, many of whom are Hong Kong or Taiwanese entrepreneurs.

But this situation is fundamentally changing. WTO accession requirements obligate China to lower tariff barriers, and between now and 2006, most restrictions on domestic market access will be phased out. Joint ventures will be required in only a few areas (such as automotive assembly but no longer engine production). Export requirements have already been eliminated. Trading rights are being vastly expanded. And foreign companies can now operate in most major economic segments—such as distribution and services—from which they were previously barred.

The resulting competition for domestic market share will be fierce, as multinationals can now look forward to competing on nearly the same terms as indigenous companies. To be sure, China will remain an exceptionally challenging environment. It is a country with inadequate legal protections, rampant intellectual property rights violations, massive government interference, severe price competition from state-subsidized firms, and other factors intimidating to the fainthearted. But Beijing's desire to expand the service and private sectors, combined with its willingness to allow foreign firms to compete nearly across the board, means that the China market, for so long just a tantalizing chimera, is now becoming a real opportunity just as the purchasing power of Chinese consumers is beginning to increase. And China is likely to remain the world's fastest growing major economy— albeit with the potential for significant growth pauses— for the coming decade and beyond.

The challenge is not only to compete successfully in China's growing domestic market but also to use the country's resources to compete in the region and around the world. In a rapidly mounting number of sectors, multinationals are finding that moving part of the value chain to China can lower costs sufficiently to make a competitive difference worldwide. Companies like Wal-Mart are already effectively leveraging their China operations both for sales in the country and for sourcing for the Western market. Every CEO must consider what competitors will do with access to the resources, the increased sales volume, and the reduced unit costs that the China market will offer. For at least the next decade, understanding how to do well in China and with Chinese resources will become a critical component in a global competitive strategy.

China thus presents two major business opportunities. For the first time, multinationals can actually go after the Chinese domestic market—and it's worth going after. And improvements in China's infrastructure, human capital, and regulatory environment are making it possible for companies to lower their costs and reap new regional and global competitive advantage. For example, Motorola is using its China facilities for research, product development, and sales to make it cost competitive in the American, European, and Asian markets. At the same time, the Chinese market itself is the most profitable piece of Motorola's global business.

Where the Risks Are

To address China's potential, we must go beyond a broad, overly optimistic look at the country; plans motivated solely by optimism and momentum too often produce regret, not profit. The risks of operating in China need to be analyzed in a hard-nosed way. Some of those risks are subtle and multifaceted. Some are distinctly unique to Chinese culture and politics. Some are present almost everywhere. None can be ignored.

THE POLITICS OF WTO IMPLEMENTATION

China's WTO accession package was negotiated by the top pro-reform leaders in the national government, who consulted very little with the parties that would be most affected, namely the telecom and other industrial ministries, as well as the provinces and cities where new foreign competition could create serious problems for local businesses. China did not even produce a Chinese-language text of the final agreement until about a month after formally acceding to the WTO in December 2001. The reality is that few localities in China are fully prepared to take on the mandated obligations, and the politics surrounding WTO implementation will be very rough.

The Chinese leaders who negotiated the WTO agreement stepped down from power in March 2003. A different leadership group will now have to decide how to implement the agreement. The potential for resulting frictions is high. The SARS epidemic has increased the likelihood of infighting by providing ammunition to those who would argue that China should slow down its pursuit of economic growth (and, implicitly, reform) and devote more attention to providing public goods like health care. The WTO obligations will probably be fully implemented, but the process is now likely to be more protracted and contentious than originally thought. Many companies will have to fight for implementation of the rules crucial to their business rather than simply assume that implementation will occur as a matter of course. And U.S.-China trade frictions are likely to rise, as China's exports to the United States continue to grow while U.S. firms point to Beijing's failures in implementing WTO obligations in such sensitive areas as opening up China's agricultural market to American exports.

OVERSUPPLY AND DEFLATION

China's underlying formula for growth has depended on a closed domestic financial system. It worked by channeling individual savings (roughly 40% of GDP) into state-owned banks, which in turn have funneled most of these funds into state-owned enterprises. They have used the money to expand capacity, despite an oversupply in many markets. This has been done to avoid the social shock of shutting down the major state-run companies, a move deemed politically too painful, considering that many smaller ones have already been shut down or privatized and tens of millions of workers laid off. The predictable results are a combination of rapid GDP growth, rising output, declining retail prices, and high levels of loan defaults. Because the major state-owned enterprises need not show a profit to survive in a soft loan environment, price competition in the domestic market has reached ruinous levels for many goods.

That growth formula will have to change. The WTO agreement requires that China permit foreign banks to offer a full range of services by 2006. This will give many individuals alternatives to putting their money into the current bankrupt system. The foreign banks will also go after the attractive business of making loans to the private sector and the more solvent state-run companies. Managing this transition will require reform of commercial banking and large state-owned companies, which will be both technically difficult and politically perilous. This situation will increase opportunities for multinational corporations in both commercial and investment banking services but will also increase the risk of instability (financial and otherwise) and potentially result in a somewhat lower growth rate, at least for a while.

THE CONSTANCY OF CHANGE

Many analysts hail each new reform in China, but the reality is that change is causing several problems for business. Last March, for example, the government set up a new Ministry of Commerce, a new banking supervision commission, and a new commission to manage state-owned assets. Months later, these agencies were still assembling their staffs and defining their missions. Constantly changing regulations, bureaucracies, and reporting relationships make business planning difficult in a country where the government continues to play a major role in the economy. WTO implementation will keep such changes the order of the day. The Chinese environment will thus remain uncomfortably fluid for purposes of forward planning. And missteps leading to a financial crisis must be considered an underlying risk.

THE STRUCTURE OF POLITICAL POWER

Basically, the fastest way for a leader at the local level to rise to a higher position is to oversee successful economic growth in the locality (township, county, city, and province) under his control. This has produced a lot of de facto flexibility and initiative at all levels, even in an authoritarian system with a socialist planning heritage. But it has also led many local governments to impose protectionist measures to reduce competition from other parts of the country and abroad. Consequently, for example, China's intellectual property rights protections, although strong in theory, are in fact almost impossible to enforce in much of the country. Local governments protect their own counterfeiting operations as sources of local revenue. Moreover, there are no constitutional rules that define the division of authority between different levels of the political system. That division is based on policy rather than law, and policies change constantly.

POTENTIAL FOR SERIOUS DISRUPTION

China's recent political succession for the first time in more than a century took place on time and peacefully. But it is not complete, and the SARS epidemic has complicated the process of sorting out authority among different groups in the new leadership. The Chinese system works well only when the top leaders are able to manage their differences unobtrusively. Open disagreement at the top produces policy stagnation and increases the chances that social discontent will erupt into large-scale political instability.

The new leaders of China also face enormous challenges in deciding on the extremely difficult trade-offs involved in allocating the country's scarce resources to address, among others, the following compelling demands:

- nonperforming loans in the state-owned banking system, which are likely to total more than $500 billion;

- an underfunded social safety net and a shortfall in investment in public goods such as health care services (funds needed to set up the pension system alone may total $500 billion);

- expensive ongoing and proposed environmental projects to relieve severe growth bottlenecks, such as the acute water shortage on the North China Plain;

- financially beleaguered town and county governments, roughly 90% of which are so burdened with unfunded mandates and resulting debt incurred to cover their obligations that they are effectively bankrupt.

The threats of unemployment, social unrest, and financial crisis place a premium on sustaining rapid economic growth. It is too early to tell whether the new government leaders will be able to work together effectively enough to make and implement the tough decisions on the national agenda.

Advice to CEOs

Every company and industry is different, but the quarter-century of experience that multinationals have had in

China points to some enduring lessons. A company's expansion into China moves through three broad phases: entry, country development, and global integration. Each of these stages has distinct goals, organizational requirements, and challenges. (See the exhibit "The Three Phases of Investment.")

During the first phase, a company's initial entry into China, the key goals are to establish a presence, begin to build a brand, and learn about the operating environment. The managers best suited to this early phase have typically done start-up work in other developing countries. They're very good at working in unstructured environments; they can take creative approaches to pulling together resources; they assume they will find much confusion in the operating environment. China today is much more business ready than it was, but making sense of the complex situation for obtaining approvals, establishing an office, and choosing vendors and advisers often requires improvisation and haggling skills that many otherwise top-notch managers simply do not have.

The second phase, country development, is prolonged, complex, and requires different managerial talents. The small representative office in which the company set up shop becomes part of a network of serious business initiatives, generally involving more than one operating division. The company should be more fully establishing its brand, developing a market, and following a geographic expansion strategy. The make-do country manager who was so suited to phase one is liable to be a disaster in this phase. As several divisions and many functions start operating in China, coordination problems with the home office begin to emerge. The operation is now becoming important enough to provide regional, and potentially global, benefits to the firm, and

The Three Phases of Investment

A multinational corporation's operations in China evolve through three distinct periods, each with characteristic goals, structures, and management needs.

	Entry	Country Development	Global Integration
Key goals:	· Determine the right business model: -Use China as a manufacturing base? -Sell into China? · Establish a presence: -Choose locality -Select partner (or establish wholly foreign-owned enterprise) -Learn domestic operating environment	· Expand operation to several initiatives and several localities · Coordinate lobbying and negotiation with Chinese government across business units: articulate "one face to China" · Seek positive P&L results	· Establish full integration of China operations into regional and global efforts
Role of the China office:	· Establish the corporate brand with local and national government · Provide services to business units as they enter the China market	· Build brand awareness with customers · Manage coordination between business units and local governments · Lead "one face to China" strategy with Chinese government · Manage awareness of China operation at corporate headquarters	· Further integrate China operations into regional and global strategy
Ideal China manager profile:	· Entrepreneurial manager who is creative and flexible · Experienced starting operations in developing countries	· Senior manager with strong ties to leadership at corporate headquarters · Experienced in communicating across complex corporate matrix	· Senior manager able to work with several business divisions

it's during this phase that headquarters wants positive P&L numbers from China. Yet despite increasing elements of transnational integration, the company will still need a strong strategy focused specifically on succeeding in China's business environment and political context.

In the third phase, mainland China–based operations are fully integrated into regional and global efforts, in the way Hong Kong or Singapore operations are. China becomes a "normal" location with particular resources, rather than a place that requires a specialized country effort. A handful of Western companies have reached this stage for narrow parts of their China efforts, primarily on the R&D side. But none has as yet arrived at this phase for its whole operation.

Because most Western multinationals now find themselves moving into the second phase, country development, the discussion that follows focuses on issues that become salient then. What are the strategic and managerial challenges in this phase of a company's operations in China? Our research suggests five that are important enough to be labeled "success factors."

FOCUS ATTENTION ON PROPERLY NESTING YOUR CHINA EFFORT INTO THE ORGANIZATION AS A WHOLE

During the entry phase, a multinational's business divisions generally work independently, as each pursues its own approach to China. The company's China country office struggles to influence the operations of the business divisions and to be treated as more than just a staff office that arranges for appointments, briefings, and hotel rooms. But in phase two, as they expand and shift into country development, smart companies quickly learn the value of establishing a strong, first-rate country office that exercises substantial control over corporate strategy and China operations. (By contrast, business divisions will again play a larger role when the company moves into stage three, the global integration phase.)

Most global corporations currently downplay country management, putting more power in the hands of business unit and product line managers. China begs to be the exception to this practice, at least for now. Business unit autonomy does not work well there because the Chinese government views corporations as single entities and largely treats them as such.

Instead, it pays to show "one face to China"—that is, to establish a corporate identity that highlights the compatibility between the company's goals and the country's goals. This can help enormously in obtaining critical licenses, regulatory decisions, and other actions that can dramatically affect the company's fortunes. A corporation is seen as a single entity when such high-level favors are granted. So in considering which favors to seek, the company needs to coordinate and set priorities among the demands of its operating divisions to avoid expending political capital on secondary matters. What's more, Beijing views concessions it wins from any division as concessions it can demand of all divisions in China. That can create very unpleasant surprises if the effort is not properly coordinated across the entire company.

These considerations argue for establishing a strong China headquarters and possibly shifting a significant part of overall P&L responsibility to the China office. The China office should participate in negotiations for all new ventures, in all national-level government relations, and in all strategic planning for the company's China effort.

Firms have struggled to find fully satisfactory ways of nesting their China efforts into the corporate matrix. Internal politics are inevitably difficult, as product line managers fail to see why they are autonomous everywhere except in China. Generally, it is important that a senior person head the China office—someone with good personal ties to the corporate CEO—so that problems with global business divisions can be addressed with the requisite authority. That person must work closely with the head of each pertinent global and geographical management unit, but if she or he must go through these individuals to communicate with the CEO and the board of directors, the China strategy is likely to encounter big trouble.

Serious China efforts are expensive and important enough to warrant direct contact from top corporate officers, including the board, which should meet in China every few years. This helps the company keep sight of how the possibilities in China relate to larger corporate goals and also helps senior executives understand the country well enough to appreciate the sometimes peculiar ways their firm needs to operate there to be successful.

TAILOR STRATEGIES FOR BOTH THE NATIONAL LEVEL AND EACH LOCALITY

While the national level requires the "one face to China" approach, each local level demands separate analysis and attention within that framework. In this sense, operating in China is not unlike operating in the United States, whose multitiered government structure has long baffled newcomers. In China, though, all levels of government are more intrusive and less bound by law and regulations than they are in the States.

Localities differ enormously in the quality of their governments and workforces, their experience with international business practices, their regulatory environments, consumer demand and preferences, and even the degree to which their local economies are dominated by state-owned or private enterprises. What works well in one place will almost certainly need to be modified to work elsewhere.

It is extremely important both to correctly identify differences in government and consumer preferences in each locality and to develop the expertise to lobby government at every level. For example, foreign firms initially depended on courts to implement the trademark law. Weaknesses in the court system led firms to lobby national and local government agencies to bolster enforcement. But continuing failures have led companies to deepen their lobbying efforts with individual local governments to persuade them to bring actual criminal charges against trademark violators.

Some have argued that developing personal ties—called *guanxi* in Chinese—is sufficient for success. They are wrong. Guanxi can be very helpful but are not enough. Officials change position, fall out of favor, or simply promise more than they can deliver. There is no substitute for developing a good understanding of the market and producing a competitive product. Still, the fact remains that despite all the market-oriented reforms, Chinese officials retain the capacity to undermine the profitability of a company, even one with excellent fundamentals, if they wish. Knowing which officials need to be supportive and how to develop helpful relations with them is therefore an integral part of a successful business strategy. At least some of the firm's executives must make the ongoing efforts necessary for effective relationship building.

ADOPT A "SHOW ME" ATTITUDE TOWARD THE PURPORTED ADVANTAGES OF FORMING A JOINT VENTURE

Even though forming a joint venture is no longer the only legal way a company can operate in China, the pressure to find joint-venture partners remains strong, particularly as companies expand their activities into more regions of the country. Often, local governments ask foreign firms to establish joint ventures in order to enter the local market. Although China looks like a huge single market, it is for the most part an assortment of local and regional markets, each requiring its own operating presence. Automotive assemblers in different regions, for example, source their parts overwhelmingly from local suppliers. Delphi has, accordingly, set up more than a dozen ventures in various places. The local partner can provide existing facilities, knowledge of the local government, and a Chinese face in the area.

But joint ventures, difficult in any country, are especially so in China. Government officials often promote ailing Chinese companies as candidates. Even very capable Chinese partners may prove problematic. For example, most multinationals want to reinvest profits so they can expand into additional domestic markets, but most

Chinese firms, which typically are cash strapped and have a more parochial mind-set, want to dominate their local market and then take profits out. The foreign company seeks peak efficiency; the Chinese partner, sensitive to the government's social goals, often looks for ways to maintain and even expand its current labor force. Understanding the quality, style, and goals of the partner's top management is crucial. Occupying the same bed while dreaming different dreams rarely produces a sustainable marriage.

Setting up what the Chinese call "a wholly foreign-owned enterprise" as an independent legal entity is, therefore, increasingly the way to go. The WFOE can provide management control—a serious issue given the shortage of top-notch Chinese managers and the divergent goals of most Chinese and foreign managers. It also affords somewhat better protection of intellectual property rights, because in a WFOE no Chinese manager need have access to full information about the firm's production processes. WFOEs are now permitted in most sectors, and many companies have found that the only way to pursue their national corporate strategy in China is to buy out their previous partners and convert the joint venture into a WFOE.

RECOGNIZE AND TAKE STEPS TO LIMIT THE PARTICULAR RISKS OF OPERATING IN THE CHINESE ENVIRONMENT

Some risks cannot be managed. The potential persists for major social and political unrest. Political frictions at the top, for instance, could prevent the government from taking effective measures to deal with some escalating financial crisis that could ultimately produce runs on the banks, riots, and a cascading breakdown of authority and order. Should that occur, few firms will escape without serious losses.

But shy of a major breakdown, risk can be managed. First, hire or develop experts who can penetrate the Chinese system enough to recognize when tensions are growing, understand the issues being contested internally, and work out strategies to move critical regulatory decisions forward.

Second, do not put all the company's resources for a critical operation in China. No single place is completely safe from natural or political disaster. SARS spread in the Pearl River Delta for months before the problem was publicly recognized. The governments of Shenyang and Xiamen were largely paralyzed when Beijing subjected them to massive corruption investigations. Geographic and political dispersion is important, even when there are cost savings to concentration.

Third, keep out of China critical technologies and production processes that can be pirated. There are many defenses against violations of intellectual property rights, such as compartmentalizing production know-how, opting for a WFOE rather than a joint venture, and highly automating the manufacture of complex products. But it is a basic reality that the Chinese have demonstrated a huge capacity for theft of intellectual property in everything from computer programs and compact discs to automobiles and designer jeans. For many operations, the safest way to mitigate the risk is to keep one very sensitive part of the production process outside the country.

Finally, because China's operating environment is difficult, rapidly changing, and fairly risky, it is important to make periodic risk assessments of your China operations so you can be prepared, if necessary, to move some operations elsewhere.

AVOID IRRATIONAL EXUBERANCE IN RESPONDING TO THE OPPORTUNITIES CHINA PRESENTS

Like items in a shop window, China's attractions are changing over time. The country's advantage in manufacturing for the export markets is well known and becoming increasingly well established. And the big news about post-WTO China is, of course, the opening of its domestic market. What's more, a third major draw is just starting to emerge. Creative companies such as General Motors, Microsoft, and Motorola have begun leveraging China's engineering power and R&D expertise to reduce new-product development costs for products sold both in country and abroad.

Each of these opportunities carries different investment and management implications. So various business units of the same company may be pursuing separate opportunities and bringing different goals to the company's China effort. It is important to sort through the operational consequences of these different efforts and set clear goals to guide each unit's thinking about such fundamentals as where to set up shop and how to evaluate progress.

Using China as an export base, for example, is very likely to dictate a coastal operation, probably in the Pearl or Yangtze River Deltas. For local high-end consumer sales, Beijing/Tianjin, the Shanghai area, and the Guangzhou region are the richest markets. But there is already enormous competition for the limited number of high-end consumers. Those multinationals that can learn how to lower production costs enough to compete for the large majority of the population further down the economic pyramid can find major new markets in China and employ those production methods competitively in similar markets elsewhere.[1] This requires a company to establish operations farther inland.

The numbers associated with China—22% of the world's population, the fastest growing major economy in the world over the past quarter century, the largest recipient of foreign direct investment last year—too often blind corporate leaders to the country's difficult business topography and the stronger business opportunities available elsewhere. Not all industries will find a source of competitive advantage in China. India, for example, is uniquely competitive in segments that do not require extensive physical infrastructure and are not encumbered by its notorious regulatory restrictions. Software services, design work, call centers, insurance claims, and other customer account services all fall into this category. India's large cadre of well-trained, fluent English speakers is a strategic resource. China does not match India's advantages in these areas. Tough-minded analyses that pinpoint why to go to China, where to locate there, and what to do elsewhere should not be given short shrift in a rush to plant the flag. (See "Twenty Questions About Your China Strategy and Operations" at the end of this article.)

CHINA'S RAPID GROWTH, expanding openness, developing consumer market, and large, low-cost, and increasingly well-trained labor force are making it a global focal point for foreign direct investment. Firms that take advantage of what China offers should reduce their costs and expand their sales in ways that provide advantage not only in China but also regionally and globally.

But CEOs need to understand the implications of China's current stage of development for their particular companies. Many who fail in China do so because they have been too fuzzy about their goals; inattentive to the difficulties of nesting a China effort within the firm; insufficiently diligent in considering potential partners, locations, and expansion plans; unwilling to make the hard choices necessary to establish one face to China; and not mindful of the strategies available to mitigate the inherent risks in a significant China play. China is a major opportunity for both increased domestic sales and greater competitive advantage elsewhere for those who forthrightly face up to its complexities. It will remain largely inscrutable—and unprofitable—for the rest.

Twenty Questions About Your China Strategy and Operations

IS YOUR CHINA STRATEGY EFFECTIVE? Answer these questions and see.

Nesting China operations into the business as a whole

Does your China office have substantial control in crafting the corporate China strategy?

Has the China office developed and executed a "one face to China" strategy that all your business divisions in China follow?

Is the China office a partner in all negotiations with the Chinese government?

Does your China office have a significant portion of the P&L responsibility for your China operations?

Is the China effort led by a senior manager who has personal and direct ties to the global leaders of your company?

Have you taken measures to assure that the board of directors remains well informed about your China effort?

Tailoring strategies to both national and local governments and markets

Do you have distinct national and local strategies?

Has each operational locality been analyzed and a local strategy crafted? Does your strategy:

- reflect awareness of practices and priorities of local government?
- consider local labor force strengths and weaknesses?
- identify local market characteristics?

Have efforts been made to develop the ability to lobby the government at each level?

Evaluating the choice between a JV and WFOE

Do you understand the management capabilities and goals of a potential JV partner?

Have the benefits and risks of operating a new venture as a JV versus a WFOE been weighed carefully?

Have you explored the option of buying out an underperforming JV partner?

Minimizing China-specific risks

Have you avoided putting all your critical operations in one locality?

Have you brought on board China expertise to help identify internal tensions and develop pertinent responses?

Have you either kept critical intellectual property out of China entirely or taken other measures to avoid piracy losses?

Matching means to ends without irrational exuberance

If you are using China as an export base, have you considered locating your operation in a coastal region to take advantage of its unique strengths?

If you are trying to sell in China, have you thought carefully about tailoring products and plant locations so you can sell to second-tier consumers?

Have you fully assessed whether to put operations in countries that may be more suitable for your needs?

If starting up in China, do you know exactly why you are going to China and what you should be able to achieve there?

Have you planned for management succession through the evolution and growth of your China operation?

Notes

1. This issue is discussed in some detail in "The End of Corporate Imperialism," by C.K. Prahalad and Kenneth Lieberthal, a classic 1998 HBR article reprinted in the August 2003 issue. It is further explored in "Serving the World's Poor, Profitably," by Prahalad and Allen Hammond (HBR September 2002).

Originally published in October 2003
Reprint R0310D

The Chinese Negotiation

JOHN L. GRAHAM AND N. MARK LAM

Executive Summary

MOST WESTERNERS PREPARING for a business trip to China like to arm themselves with a list of etiquette how-tos. "Carry a boatload of business cards," tipsters say. "Bring your own interpreter." "Speak in short sentences." "Wear a conservative suit." Such advice can help get companies in the door and even through the first series of business transactions. But it won't sustain the prolonged, year-in, year-out associations Chinese and Western businesses can now achieve.

The authors' work with dozens of companies and thousands of American and Chinese executives over the past 20 years has demonstrated that a superficial adherence to etiquette rules gets executives only so far. They have witnessed communication breakdowns between American and Chinese businesspeople time and time again. The root cause: the American side's failure to understand the much broader context of Chinese culture and values, a problem that too often leaves Western negotiators flummoxed and flailing.

American and Chinese approaches often appear incompatible. Americans see Chinese negotiators as inefficient, indirect, and even dishonest, while the Chinese see American negotiators as aggressive, impersonal, and excitable. Such perceptions have deep cultural origins. Yet those who know how to navigate these differences can develop thriving, mutually profitable, and satisfying business relationships.

Four cultural threads have bound the Chinese people together for some 5,000 years, and these show through in Chinese business negotiations. They are agrarianism, morality, the Chinese pictographic language, and wariness of strangers. Most Western businesspeople often find those elements mysterious and confusing. But ignore them at any time during the negotiation process, and the deal can easily fall apart.

IN PREPARING FOR A business trip to China, most Westerners like to arm themselves with a handy, one-page list of etiquette how-tos. "Carry a boatload of business cards," tipsters say. "Bring your own interpreter." "Speak in short sentences." "Wear a conservative suit." Such advice can help get you in the door and even through the first series of business transactions. But it won't sustain the kind of prolonged, year-in, year-out associations that Chinese and Western businesses can now achieve.

Indeed, our work with dozens of companies and thousands of American and Chinese executives over the past 20 years has demonstrated to us that a superficial obedience to the rules of etiquette gets you only so far. In fact, we have witnessed breakdowns between American and Chinese businesspeople time and time again. The root cause: a failure on the American side to understand the much broader context of Chinese culture and values, a problem that too often leaves Western negotiators both flummoxed and flailing.

The challenge of mutual understanding is great; American and Chinese approaches often appear incompatible. All too often, Americans see Chinese negotiators as inefficient, indirect, and even dishonest, while the Chinese see American negotiators as aggressive, impersonal, and excitable. Such differences have deep cultural origins. Yet those who know how to navigate these differences can develop thriving, mutually profitable, and satisfying business relationships.

Several caveats before we continue: First, we use Americans as our primary examples of Western negotiators not only because our research has focused primarily on U.S. companies and executives but also because Americans exhibit individualism and assertiveness more strongly than other Westerners do. As a result, they tend to get into more trouble at the negotiating table. Second, we acknowledge that our sweeping statements about a billion-plus people can be simplistic. (We admit to stereotyping Americans, too.) Nevertheless, we are confident in asserting that the cultural values discussed here apply, in varying degrees, to most Chinese—whether they live in China or in other parts of the world. Finally, the Chinese reader will not be surprised by what we observe here. Our goal is to help Western and Chinese negotiators learn to work together more efficiently with mutual respect and gain the ultimate prizes. (See "The View from Both Sides" for more information.)

The View from Both Sides

American	Chinese

THEIR BASIC CULTURAL VALUES AND WAYS OF THINKING

American	Chinese
individualist	collectivist
egalitarian	hierarchical
information oriented	relationship oriented
reductionist	holistic
sequential	circular
seeks the truth	seeks the way
the argument culture	the haggling culture

HOW THEY APPROACH THE NEGOTIATION PROCESS

Nontask Sounding

American	Chinese
quick meetings	long courting process
informal	formal
make cold calls	draw on intermediaries

Information Exchange

American	Chinese
full authority	limited authority
direct	indirect
proposals first	explanations first

Means of Persuasion

American	Chinese
aggressive	questioning
impatient	enduring

Terms of Agreement

American	Chinese
forging a "good deal"	forging a long-term relationship

The Roots of Chinese Culture

Four thick threads of culture have bound the Chinese people together for some 5,000 years, and these show through in Chinese business negotiations.

The first thread is agrarianism. In contrast to the U.S. population, which is mostly urban, two-thirds of the Chinese people still live in rural areas, laboring primarily in rice or wheat cultivation. Traditional Chinese agriculture is peasant farming. It is communal, not individualistic; survival depends on group cooperation and harmony. Loyalty and obedience to familial hierarchy binds laboring groups together. Many of China's city dwellers were born and raised in the country and have retained their agrarian values. Just as the most urbane Americans are influenced by the country's cowboy roots—"shoot first and ask questions later," "lay your cards on the table," and so on—the most modern Chinese are affected by millennia of living close to the soil.

Before the 1980s, agrarian values trumped business values. When during the Cultural Revolution Mao Tse-tung sent bureaucrats and students to be "reeducated" by the peasantry, he was reflecting the deep-seated belief in the virtues of rural life. Indeed, Chinese philosopher Fung Yu-lan explains in his works that Chinese sages historically distinguished between the "root" (agriculture) and the "branch" (commerce). Social and economic theories and policies tended to favor the root and slight the branch. People who dealt with the branch—merchants—were therefore looked down upon.

The second thread is morality. The writings of Confucius served as the foundation of Chinese education for some 2,000 years. During those two millennia, knowledge of Confucian texts was the primary requisite for appointment to government offices. Confucius maintained that a society organized under a benevolent moral code would be prosperous and politically stable and therefore safe from attack. He also taught reverence for scholarship and kinship. Confucius defined five cardinal relationships: between ruler and ruled, husband and wife, parents and children, older and younger brothers, and friend and friend. Except for the last, all the relationships were strictly hierarchical. The ruled—wives, children, and younger brothers—were counseled to trade obedience and loyalty for the benevolence of their rulers—husbands, parents, and older brothers. Rigorous adherence to these hierarchical relationships yielded social harmony, the antidote for the violence and civil war of Confucius's time.

For a taste of the importance of hierarchy in Chinese society, consider what happened to Cheng Han-cheng and his wife. According to Chinese scholar Dau-lin Hsu, in 1865 Cheng's wife had the insolence to beat her mother-in-law. This was regarded as such a heinous crime that, among other punishments, Cheng and his wife were both skinned alive, their flesh displayed at the gates of various cities, and their bones burned to ashes. Neighbors and extended family members were also punished. This is, of course, an extreme example—but the story is oft told, even in today's China. And it underscores why it is so easy for casual Westerners to slight their authority-revering Chinese counterparts.

Roughly contemporary with Confucius was Lao Tsu, the inspiration for Taoism, whose fundamental notions involve the relationship of yin (the feminine, dark, and passive force) to yang (the masculine, light, and active force). The two forces oppose and complement one another simultaneously. They cannot be separated but must be considered as a whole. The implications of the collision and collusion of yin and yang are pervasive, affecting every aspect of life from traditional medicine to economic cycles. According to Lao Tsu, the key to life was to find the Tao—"the way" between the two forces, the middle ground, a compromise. Both Lao Tsu and Confucius were less concerned about finding the truth and more concerned about finding the way.

These moral values express themselves in the Chinese negotiating style. Chinese negotiators are more concerned with the means than the end, with the process more than the goal. The best compromises are derived only through the ritual back-and-forth of haggling. This process cannot be cut short. And a compromise allows the two sides to hold equally valid positions. While Americans tend to believe that the truth, as they see it, is worth arguing over and even getting angry about, the Chinese believe that the way is hard to find and so rely on haggling to settle differences.

The third cultural thread is the Chinese pictographic language. Just as Western children learn to read Roman letters and numbers at an early age, Chinese children learn to memorize thousands of pictorial characters. Because, in Chinese, words are pictures rather than sequences of letters, Chinese thinking tends toward a more holistic processing of information. Michael Harris Bond, a psychology professor at the Chinese University of Hong Kong, found that Chinese children are better at seeing the big picture, while American children have an easier time focusing on the details.

The fourth thread is the Chinese people's wariness of foreigners, which has been learned the hard way—from the country's long and violent history of attacks from all points of the compass. So, too, has China fallen victim to internal squabbling, civil wars, and the ebb and flow of empires. The combination yields cynicism about the rule of law and rules in general. It can be said that the Chinese trust in only two things: their families and their bank accounts.

The Eight Elements

The cultural influences outlined above have given rise to a clearly defined set of elements that underpins the Chinese negotiation style. Most American businesspeople we have worked with often find those elements mysterious and confusing. But if Americans ignore them at any time during the negotiation process, the deal can easily fall apart—as American businessman John Shipwright found out. (While his story is true, his identity has been disguised.)

Shipwright, an oil industry sales executive, traveled to Shanghai to nail what he believed was already a done deal. He was well briefed by the team that had begun the negotiation, armed with a handy pamphlet about Chinese business practices and etiquette, and bolstered by friends' advice. On day one, John followed their counsel to the letter, including treating his Chinese customers to an expensive dinner, which the pamphlet also recommended. On day two, he was invited to their offices, where he discussed every aspect of his company's offer, including delivery. Afterward, he treated his customers to another pricey repast.

On day three, the Chinese again asked about delivery. Shipwright repeated his company's stipulations, and the two sides discussed a variety of the other issues. On day four, having asked Shipwright to repeat the information about delivery yet another time, the customers agreed to an order-to-installation cycle that would take six months, and Shipwright considered the negotiations wrapped up. Day five found John eagerly anticipating his trip home, but that excitement gave way to dismay when the customers reiterated their question about delivery. That's when Shipwright snapped. Visibly reddening, he blurted, "What? You want to talk about delivery *again*?" Taken aback by the outburst, the Chinese customers asked the interpreter what was wrong. They adjourned the meeting without comment and without arranging for another meeting. Two months later when he was back in Houston, Shipwright learned that those customers had inked a deal with a competitor.

Shipwright's outburst may have killed his deal, but that's not what really went wrong. His problem was deeper: He misunderstood the fundamentals of negotiating in China. Following are the eight important elements of the Chinese negotiation style in the order most Westerners will encounter them.

GUANXI (PERSONAL CONNECTIONS)

In fact, "personal connections" doesn't do justice to the fundamental, and complex, concept of *guanxi*. While Americans put a premium on networking, information, and institutions, the Chinese place a premium on individuals' social capital within their group of friends, relatives, and close associates. Though the role of guanxi is fading a bit against the backdrop of population mobility and the Westernization of some Chinese business practices, it remains an important social force. More often than not, the person with the best guanxi wins.

Here's an example of how guanxi works. Upon learning that China Post Savings Bureau planned to modernize its computer network, C.T. Teng, the general manager of Honeywell-Bull's Greater China Region, asked his

Beijing sales director to approach the China Post executive responsible for this project. Because the sales director and the China Post executive were old university
friends, they had guanxi. That connection enabled Teng
to invite the China Post executive to a partner's forum at
Honeywell-Bull headquarters in Boston. He also invited
the CEO of Taiwan's Institute of Information Industry to
the event. Over the course of the meeting, Teng proposed
a banking system using Honeywell-Bull hardware and
Taiwan Institute software to China Post's CEO, and the
deal was accepted.

Good guanxi also depends on a strict system of
reciprocity, or what the Chinese call *hui bao*. This does
not mean immediate, American-style reciprocity: "I
make a concession, and I expect one in return at the
table that day." In China, there's no hurry; agrarian
rhythms run long. Favors are almost always remembered
and returned, though not right away. This long-term
reciprocity is a cornerstone of enduring personal relationships. Ignoring reciprocity in China is not just bad
manners; it's immoral. If someone is labeled *wang' en
fuyi* (one who forgets favors and fails on righteousness
and loyalty), it poisons the well for all future business.

ZHONGJIAN REN (THE INTERMEDIARY)

Business deals for Americans in China don't have a
chance without the *zhongjian ren*, the intermediary. In
the United States, we tend to trust others until or unless
we're given reason not to. In China, suspicion and dis-
trust characterize all meetings with strangers. In business, trust can't be earned because business relationships can't even be formed without it. Instead, trust must
be transmitted via guanxi. That is, a trusted business

associate of yours must pass you along to his trusted business associates. In China, the crucial first step in this phase of negotiation, called "nontask sounding," is finding the personal links to your target organization or executive.

Those links can be hometown, family, school, or previous business ties. What's crucial is that the links be based on personal experience. For example, you call your former classmate and ask him to set up a dinner meeting with his friend. Expensive meals at nice places are key. If things go well, his friend accepts the role of zhongjian ren and in turn sets up a meeting with your potential client or business partner, whom he knows quite well.

A talented Chinese go-between is indispensable even after the initial meeting takes place. Consider what happens during a typical Sino-Western negotiation session. Rather than just saying no outright, Chinese businesspeople are more likely to change the subject, turn silent, ask another question, or respond by using ambiguous and vaguely positive expressions with subtle negative implications, such as *hai bu cuo* ("seems not wrong"), *hai hao* ("seems fairly all right"), and *hai xing* or *hai ke yi* ("appears fairly passable").

Only a native Chinese speaker can read and explain the moods, intonations, facial expressions, and body language Chinese negotiators exhibit during a formal negotiation session. Frequently, only the zhongjian ren can determine what's going on. When an impatient Westerner asks what the Chinese think of a proposal, the respondents will invariably offer to *kan kan* or *yanjiu yanjiu*, which means, "Let us take a look," or "Let us study it"—even if they think the proposal stinks. This is where the zhongjian ren can step in because he is an interpreter not so much of words as of cultures. Often, the two parties can say frankly to the intermediary what they cannot say to each other. In China, the intermediary—not the negotiator—first brings up the business issue to be discussed. And the intermediary often settles differences. Indeed, we have seen more than one zhongjian ren successfully deal with divisive disagreements. The following is one such case.

A vice president of a New York–based software company went to Beijing to negotiate a distribution contract with a Chinese research institute. Having attended meetings arranged by the intermediary—a former senior executive with the institute—the VP was pleased with the progress during the first two days. But on the third day, the two sides became embroiled in a fruitless debate over intellectual property rights. Feeling they were losing face, the Chinese ended the meeting. That night, the VP and the China country manager met with the intermediary. The following day, the intermediary called the head of the institute and worked his magic. In the end, both sides agreed that the intellectual property rights were to be jointly owned, and the contract was signed.

SHEHUI DENGJI (SOCIAL STATUS)

Westerners frequently find it difficult to understand the formality of Chinese businesspeople. American-style, "just call me Mary" casualness does not play well in a country where the Confucian values of obedience and deference to one's superiors remain strong. The formality goes much deeper, however—unfathomably so, to many Westerners.

Consider what happened when one U.S. company neglected to pay attention to the importance of *shehui dengji* in Chinese culture. The company sent a relatively young and low-level sales representative to a high-level negotiation. The Chinese executive remarked, "Ah, you're about the same age as my son." The Chinese felt insulted by the Americans' failure to send an executive whose rank at least equaled theirs. They doubted the Americans' sincerity, and the deal died before it began.

At some point, negotiations may require a meeting of equals in the hopes of stimulating more cooperation. But top-level Chinese executives will not be prepared to bargain and will not be persuaded. It's simply not their role. Rather, they will evaluate the relationship during a show of sincerity or *cheng-yi* by their Western counterparts. And high-level meetings can work wonders. When General Motors was courting Shanghai Auto back in 1995, CEO John F. Smith made three trips to Beijing to meet with Chinese executives. This is one reason you'll see Buicks traveling Beijing boulevards, not Fords. (But it's about more than the number of trips the CEO takes. It's about whom a company sends to China. See "Who's on Your Side of the Negotiating Table?" at the end of this article.)

RENJI HEXIE (INTERPERSONAL HARMONY)

The Chinese sayings, "A man without a smile should not open a shop" and "Sweet temper and friendliness produce money" speak volumes about the importance of harmonious relations between business partners. While respect and responsibility are the glue that binds hierarchical relationships, friendships and positive feelings, or *renji hexie*, hold relationships of equals together. In the United States, the initial sizing up—the nontask sounding—takes minutes. In China, nontask sounding may last days, weeks, even months. And it includes home visits, invitations to sporting or other events, and long dinners during which everything but business is discussed. There's just no other way.

All this can be hard on your liver. On the eve of negotiations between the chief executive of a U.S. firm and one from a major Chinese company, the Chinese hosted a lavish dinner at the best banquet hall in the city. The Chinese CEO proposed a toast: "Let's drink to our friendship! We will have long cooperation! But if you aren't drunk tonight, there will be no contract tomorrow." The executive from the American firm matched him drink for drink—and couldn't remember how he got back to his hotel. The next morning he was greeted with a hangover, a big smile, and a fat contract. Indeed, Chinese negotiators do not understand the Americans' haste to get the deal done. For the Chinese, any attempt to do business without having established sufficient renji hexie is rude, and they can force the issue when necessary.

For instance, a vice president of a U.S. computer maker went to Beijing hoping to close a deal with the Ministry of Education. The local sales team had been working with an intermediary on this case for more than six months, and the intermediary arranged a dinner party with a deputy education minister for the evening the vice president from the U.S. company arrived. Many toasts to mutual cooperation were made, and in accordance with what the American executive had been briefed to do, no business was discussed. The next day, the vice president paid a visit to the deputy minister. Sensing that the atmosphere was right based on the previous night's social gathering, the vice president asked, "So, when can we sign the contract?" The deputy minister politely replied, "Well, Mr. Vice President, you just arrived in Beijing. You must be tired. Why not take your time and see the city first?" It took a week of sight-seeing to get negotiations back on track.

In the final analysis, trust and harmony are more important to Chinese businesspeople than any piece of paper. Until recently, Chinese property rights and contract law were virtually nonexistent—and are still inadequate by Western standards. So it's no wonder that Chinese businesspeople rely more on good faith than on tightly drafted deals. While contracts are becoming increasingly important and more likely to be enforced now that China has joined the WTO, Chinese negotiators still insist on satisfaction with the spirit of the deal.

Interestingly, one aspect of Chinese negotiation strikes Westerners as quite impolite. This is the common Chinese tactic of threatening to do business elsewhere. It's called *liangshou zhunbei* (two-handed preparation) and carries the additional implication that the Chinese have already begun talks with competitors. Most Westerners feel insulted when Chinese negotiators talk about doing business with competitors, but the Chinese believe they are just stating the obvious and not creating reason for mistrust. This is simply part of their haggling culture.

If the Westerners do their best to maintain sufficient renji hexie, the Chinese will consider their counterparts' interests even if negotiations get rocky. When a corporate vice president of a manufacturing company threatened his Chinese counterpart with a lawsuit demanding final acceptance of a signed contract, the Chinese executive responded, "Go ahead. You may win the case. But you will be finished in the China market." At a subsequent meeting, the Greater China general manager with the manufacturing company, schooled in the Chinese style of business negotiations and possessing good renji hexie with the Chinese executive, was able to smooth things over by appealing to their mutual long-term interests. The Chinese customer responded, "This is the right attitude. I will see what I can do to expedite final acceptance."

ZHENGTI GUANNIAN (HOLISTIC THINKING)

As we have said, the Chinese think in terms of the whole while Americans think sequentially and individualistically, breaking up complex negotiation tasks into a series of smaller issues: price, quantity, warranty, delivery, and so forth. Chinese negotiators tend to talk about those issues all at once, skipping among them, and, from the Americans' point of view, seemingly never settling anything. Those Chinese negotiators who practice *zhengti guannian* want long descriptions of background and context and will ask a thousand questions.

This difference in style can frustrate Westerners accustomed to measuring progress in a linear way. To people like Shipwright, the oil industry executive, you're halfway through the negotiation when you've discussed half the issues. Americans consider the negotiations finished when they have come to the end of the list. Not so their Chinese counterparts, who feel it's at that point they can begin thinking about the package as a whole. In our experience, this difference in thinking styles is the source of the greatest tension between negotiation teams. It also often causes Americans to make unnecessary concessions right before the Chinese announce their agreement. When Tandem Computers attempted to sell its NonStop servers to China Telecom, the sales manager offered an additional 5% off the sale price if the Chinese negotiator agreed to take delivery within a month. The Chinese purchasing manager responded, "We're not really in a hurry, but since you have some room, you might as well give us the price break." For Americans bargaining in China, the message is clear: Be prepared to discuss all issues simultaneously and in an apparently haphazard order. Nothing is settled until everything is.

How then can one know if negotiations are progressing well? It is a good sign if higher-level Chinese executives attend the discussions or if their questions begin to focus on specific areas of the deal. Also, Americans should look for some recognizable softening of attitudes and positions on some issues. If they notice the Chinese increasingly talking among themselves in their own language, it could mean they're trying to decide something. Additional signs of progress include Chinese calls for more meetings, requests to bring in the intermediary, or questions about "extras" such as overseas training.

JIEJIAN (THRIFT)

China's long history of economic and political instability has taught its people to save their money, a practice known as *jiejian*. According to market research firm Euromonitor International, mainland Chinese save nearly four times as much of their household income as Americans do. The focus on savings results, in business negotiations, in a lot of bargaining over price usually through haggling.

Chinese negotiators will pad their offers with more room to maneuver than most Americans are used to, and they will make concessions on price with great reluctance and only after lengthy discussions. In fact, we have often seen Americans laugh at the Chinese base price or get angry at "unreasonable" Chinese counteroffers. To make matters worse, the Chinese are adept at using silence as a negotiating tactic. This leaves Americans in the awkward position of negotiating by asking questions, directly or through the intermediary. In defending price positions, the Chinese use patience and silence as formidable weapons against American impatience and volubility. Westerners should not be put off by aggressive first offers by the Chinese; they expect both sides to make concessions eventually, particularly on prices.

Our advice to Westerners: Instead of whispering to your colleagues, "Why are we here?" expect padded prices and ask the Chinese, "How did you come up with that amount?" If the Chinese talk about a competitive offer, then it's time to ask about which competitor and which product, delivery schedule, warranty terms, and so on. This can take time, but it pays off. Recently, we saw one Chinese counteroffer for a computer system start at $2 million; after four weeks of questions, discussions, and haggling, the final agreement came to more than $4 million in the Americans' favor.

MIANZI ("FACE" OR SOCIAL CAPITAL)

In Chinese business culture, a person's reputation and social standing rest on saving face. If Westerners cause the Chinese embarrassment or loss of composure, even unintentionally, it can be disastrous for business negotiations. The Chinese notion of saving face is closely associated with American concepts of dignity and prestige. *Mianzi* defines a person's place in his social network; it is the most important measure of social worth. Sources of face can be wealth, intelligence, attractiveness, skills, position, and, of course, good guanxi. But, while Americans tend to think in absolute terms—a person either has prestige and dignity or doesn't—the Chinese think of face in quantitative terms. Face, like money, can be earned, lost, given, or taken away.

Honeywell-Bull offers a good example of the importance of saving face. The company had won negotiation rights for an order of 100 ATMs from the Bank of China. Toward the end of the process, the bank buyer asked for deeper price cuts. To him, the sticking point wasn't just a matter of thrift. He told Honeywell-Bull representatives, "If the price isn't reduced further, I will lose face." This is Chinese for "The deal will be off, and we'll talk to your competitor." The seasoned Honeywell-Bull executive responded that he had some room to move in the bid, but the lower price would not allow for training Chinese managers in the States. The Chinese representatives then asked for a ten-minute break and came back smiling, agreeing to all the terms. In retrospect, the training program was much more important to the Chinese executive. The U.S. trip for his staff yielded him more mianzi than the requested price break.

By contrast, when those negotiating with the Chinese break promises or display anger, frustration, or aggression at the negotiation table, it results in a mutual loss of face. In the West, sometimes a mock tantrum is used as a negotiating tactic, but in China it invariably backfires one way or another. Causing the Chinese business partner who brought you to the table to lose mianzi is no mere faux pas; it's a disaster.

CHIKU NAILAO (ENDURANCE, RELENTLESSNESS, OR EATING BITTERNESS AND ENDURING LABOR)

The Chinese are famous for their work ethic. But they take diligence one step further—to endurance. Where

Americans place high value on talent as a key to success, the Chinese see *chiku nailao* as much more important and honorable. That's why Chinese children attend school 251 days per year, in contrast to the Americans' 180-day school year. Hard work, even in the worst conditions, is the ideal: Witness how Chairman Mao's 18-month Long March endeared him to the Chinese people. And that ingrained industriousness now drives the country's burgeoning free-enterprise economy.

We see Chinese diligence primarily reflected in two ways at the negotiation table. First, the Chinese will have worked harder in preparing for the negotiations than the Westerners. Second, they will expect longer bargaining sessions; throw in jet lag and late-night business entertainment, and the Westerners are in for an exhausting experience. Their Chinese counterparts know to take advantage of this.

During negotiations, we recommend three tactics to demonstrate your own chiku nailao. The first is to ask questions—for, as bargaining expert Chester Karrass suggests in *The Negotiating Game*, it's "smart to be a little bit dumb." Asking the same questions more than once—"I didn't completely understand what you meant. Can you explain that again?"—can expose weaknesses in the other side's arguments. Once this occurs, those across the table will be obligated to concede. Our Mr. Shipwright, for example, would have gotten further during the negotiation had he responded to the Chinese side's repeated demands for answers about delivery in this way: "Apparently, delivery is a key issue for you. Can you remind me again why?" The Chinese admire and respond to relentlessness.

Second, show endurance by going to great lengths to do your research and then educate your Chinese counterparts. It's important to explain your company's situation, needs, and preferences, but condescension will kill this approach, so be careful. One executive long experienced in negotiations with the Chinese says it's not a bad idea to supply Chinese customers with intelligence about your own competitors or to couch arguments in the context of "internationally recognized business practices" in the service of education. And because showing is better than telling, it's important to demonstrate prospective results. A Groupe Bull of France executive was trying to sell a smart-card system to Shanghai Pudong Development Bank, and he knew it would be a tough sale. So he arranged for his Chinese equal to come to Paris for a demonstration of the technology's maturity. The education worked: Today, some 2 million smart cards are being used in thousands of Shanghai's ATMs and point-of-sale machines, as well as in all the taxicabs.

Finally, showing patience is a sign of chiku nailao. The Chinese rarely make concessions immediately following persuasive appeals without broader consultation. Indeed, the combination of group decision making and social status (shehui dengji) can make things quite complicated on the Chinese side. Moreover, the Chinese are skilled in using delay as a persuasive tactic. Therefore, you need the full backing and understanding of your home office so you can bide your time. Meanwhile, the Chinese can use apparent lulls in the negotiation cycle to consider any new information or develop more questions. In the end, the investment in time pays off. For instance, we saw a U.S manufacturer of a retail scanner system take six trips to southern China over a one-year period to make the sale. The sale was made at a profit, but the same transaction would have taken a few quick visits in the States, if that.

Though Americans would do well to prepare a list of concessions they would be willing to make in advance of the negotiations, these should not be automatically granted at the negotiation table. Once again, Americans should emulate their Chinese counterparts and exercise patience, carefully reconsidering each concession away from the social pressure of the formal negotiations.

NEGOTIATING BUSINESS DEALS in China will remain one of the most daunting and interesting challenges facing American executives during the next few decades. Indeed, we might have said the same thing back in 1789, when Yankee clipper ships first plied the Pearl River, passing Hong Kong on the way to Canton (now Guangzhou).

Fortunately, smart Western bargainers have always made money in China—and despite the difficulties in communication, the future bodes well for the new Sino-Western business class. The Chinese are working hard to catch up and compete with Western-style enterprises. And, the historical slighting of the merchant class notwithstanding, business schools are sprouting up all over the mainland, where Chinese students are learning about concepts like corporate image, brand equity, and the ins and outs of intellectual property.

For Westerners eager to do business in China, here is the last word: Move now, and learn the rules of the game by developing the guanxi needed to grow your business there. Don't expect immediate results. Old friendships work their magic through time; every year invested in

China now will pay off in the future—because in a world of millennia-old memories, relationships of the moment need long and patient nurturing.

Who's on Your Side of the Negotiating Table?

THE PEOPLE WHO REPRESENT your company in China will make all the difference when it comes to negotiating deals and forging business relationships. More than 15 years ago, Nigel Campbell, a leading expert on business strategies in China, concluded that it was essential to have the right people participating in negotiations: Foreign companies that had Chinese-born executives driving the negotiations succeeded. Others did not.

In 1994, Ford ignored this sage advice when it appointed Jim Paulson president of Ford of China. Paulson, an affable Midwestern engineer and a lifelong Ford man, had worked on plant-related issues in several foreign countries. In trying to get an entrée for Ford into China, he faced a complex negotiation environment. Governments of both countries were embroiled in fights over intellectual property regulations. GM, Toyota, and Nissan lurked in the background. Substantial product changes needed to be negotiated. Most important, Paulson didn't possess a deep cultural understanding of his Chinese counterparts. Later, in *Time* magazine, he lamented, "We tried to find out more about how they were arriving at their decisions, but we didn't have enough Chinese-speaking people to establish close contact with the officials in Shanghai."

Meanwhile, arch competitor GM had an ace in the hole named Shirley Young. Born in Shanghai, Young spoke fluent Mandarin. Her father was a war hero. Her stepfather had served as China's ambassador to the United States, the UK, and France. Young, who had worked as a consultant to GM since 1983 and joined the company in 1988 as vice president of consumer market development, boasted an Ivy League education and a wall full of awards, including Woman of the Year for the Chinese-American Planning Council.

Young offered another advantage: She brought great *guanxi*. Even though Ford had been one step ahead in the initial bidding phase, Young was able to pass the final victory to GM. By 1997, 100,000 midsize Buick Regals had been produced at a new billion-dollar assembly plant in Shanghai.

Oddly enough, Ford had the ideal person for the job—Dr. Lawrence T. Wong. An engineer raised in China, Wong possessed all the language and cultural skills that Young had, and he was president of Ford of Taiwan. He even had the critical engineering expertise that Young lacked. Perhaps the best measure of Wong's capabilities is his current position. Since 1996 he has held the reins of the Hong Kong Jockey Club—the most important horse-racing operation in the world, with annual revenues of $12 billion, and the largest charitable donor in all of China. How could Ford, blessed with such a trump card, have overlooked him?

Eventually, Ford wised up and appointed an ethnic Chinese executive to a senior position in Beijing in 1998—Mei-Wei Cheng. In April 2001, Ford completed a 50–50 joint venture agreement with Chongqing Chang'an, China's third largest automaker, to produce 50,000 small cars. It took Ford some five years to begin recovering from its shame in Shanghai. Our subsequent interviews with executives at Shanghai Auto confirmed that the key mistake Ford made was in Dearborn; that is, not selecting someone like Larry Wong to lead Ford of China in the first place.

Originally published in October 2003
Reprint R0310E

The Hidden Dragons

MING ZENG AND PETER J. WILLIAMSON

Executive Summary

MOST MULTINATIONAL CORPORATIONS are fascinated with China. Carried away by the number of potential customers and the relatively cheap labor, firms seeking a presence in China have traditionally focused on selling products, setting up manufacturing facilities, or both. But they've ignored an important development: the emergence of Chinese firms as powerful rivals—in China and also in the global marktet.

In this article, Ming Zeng and Peter Williamson describe how Chinese companies like Haier, Legend, and Pearl River Piano have quietly managed to grab market share from older, bigger, and financially stronger rivals in Asia, Europe, and the United States.

Global managers tend to offer the usual explanations for why Chinese companies don't pose a threat: They aren't big enough or profitable enough to compete overseas, the managers say, and these primarily state-owned companies are ill-financed and ill-equipped for global competition.

As the government's policies about the private owner-ship of companies changed from forbidding the practice to encouraging it, a new breed of Chinese companies evolved. The authors outline the four types of hybrid Chinese companies that are simultaneously tackling the global market. China's *national champions* are using their advantages as domestic leaders to build global brands. The *dedicated exporters* are entering foreign markets on the strength of their economies of scale. The *competitive networks* have taken on world markets by bringing together small, specialized companies that operate in close proximity. And the *technology upstarts* are using innovations developed by China's government-owned research institutes to enter emerging sectors such as biotechnology. Zeng and Williamson identify these budding multinationals, analyze their strategies, and eval-uate their weaknesses.

Ask any global manager, and he'll wax eloquent about how Red China has transformed itself over the past 25 years into a latter-day Middle Kingdom, a busi-ness realm closer to heaven than earth. China is the fastest-growing market on the planet, after all. Between 1978 and 2002, the country's GDP grew by 9.3% annu-ally—three times faster than the American economy did—and its per capita income more than quadrupled from $231 to $940 a year. With a population of 1.3 billion, China has the most consumers in the world, too, and every company wants a piece of the action. Many multinational corporations entered the country in the decades after 1978, when the Communist government started to raise the bamboo curtain, and since China joined the World Trade Organization in December 2001, many more have swarmed into a market whose potential defies imagination.

Still, most multinationals are myopic about China. Carried away by the number of potential customers and the workforce's low wages, they've been focused on setting up manufacturing facilities or selling products there, or both. They've ignored an important development: the emergence of Chinese companies as powerful rivals—not only within China but also throughout the global market. Several Chinese companies haven't been content with rewriting the economics of manufacturing in their industries. They've created brands that have quietly grabbed market share from older, bigger, and financially stronger rivals in Asia, Europe, and the United States. For instance, the Haier Group in Qingdao, one of the world's largest manufacturers of home appliances, captured almost half of the U.S. market for small refrigerators in 2002 under its own brand name. Guangdong Galanz, which manufactures one out of every three microwave ovens in the world, last year carved out a 40% share of the European market for its eponymous brand. And China International Marine Containers (CIMC) had wrested more than 40% of the global market for refrigerated containers by 2002. If the speed with which these companies have penetrated foreign markets is any indication, Chinese brands could soon become a global force in many other industries.

So why aren't Chinese brands on corporate radar screens yet? There are three intertwined reasons: First, many global managers argue that Chinese companies

aren't big enough or profitable enough to compete overseas. The Chinese market has grown, but it has become
fragmented, partly because regional differences in
income have increased sharply since the reforms of the
last quarter century. Most companies have found that
the products they market in the prosperous coastal areas
of China are too expensive for customers in the poorer
hinterland. China's weak transportation, distribution,
and retail infrastructures also make it expensive to supply goods all over the large country. Furthermore, every
provincial government imposes taxes on goods that
aren't manufactured in the region because of the economic rivalry between China's provinces. That's why
there are many regional brands but few national brands
in the country. These factors constrain the ability of Chinese companies to grow organically, and taking over
rivals remains a slow, cumbersome, and bureaucratic
process. Consequently, Chinese companies are small by
both global and Asian standards. For instance, New
Hope Group, China's largest private-sector company, had
just $1 billion in sales in 2002. That same year, South
Korea's largest company, Samsung, reached $40 billion in
sales. And Thailand's largest private company, Charoen
Pokphand Group, reported more than $5 billion in sales.

Second, the only organizations large enough to compete on a global scale are often the state-owned enterprises. According to *Fortune*, the government owned 98
of the 100 biggest Chinese companies in 2002. Many of
these enterprises suffer losses, stay in business only
because of the monopolies they enjoy, and thus aren't
globally competitive.

Third, the status quo can't be changed easily because,
until recently, the Chinese government usually denied

private companies permission to sell equity shares in the capital market or to borrow from commercial banks. (The Chinese government officially announced that it would support the growth of private business at the 16th National Congress of the Communist Party of China held in November 2002.) However, the state often invests in the shares of public-sector companies and provides them with subsidized credit. Neither public nor private companies can become competitive in such a financial system, goes the conventional wisdom.

These arguments, however comforting they may be to global managers, aren't entirely accurate. Over the past five years, we've studied the strategies and ownership structures of more than 50 Chinese companies. Our research shows that multinational executives who don't perceive China's state-owned and privately held companies as potential competitors have missed the rise of the new breed of Chinese companies that have already succeeded in capturing some foreign markets. These hybrids evolved as the government's policies about the private ownership of companies changed— from forbidding the practice to tolerating, recognizing, and encouraging it. The companies have acquired public-sector, private, and even foreign shareholders in recent years. For instance, Qingdao municipal government, local investors, and the company's managers jointly control Haier's equity. While the Chinese government holds a majority stake in TCL Group, the country's second-largest manufacturer of TVs and mobile phones, strategic investors, such as Japan's Toshiba and Sumitomo, as well as the company's managers, also own shares. And shareholders of China's Legend Group, which last year had a 20% share of the global market for motherboards, include the Chinese Academy of Sciences, local investors, and managers. Officially, Legend is classified as "state-owned, non-government-run."

Companies like Haier, TCL, and Legend have become globally competitive because their mixed ownership allows them to overcome the weaknesses of the Chinese system. They're driven by the profit motive in what is still a Communist country, yet they receive support from one or more arms of the state. The government doesn't interfere with operations at these companies because the businesses aren't part of the public sector, and so these hybrids enjoy almost total autonomy. At the same time, government officials believe that the global success of these companies will further national, regional, and even personal interests. They've often been involved in setting up the hybrids, sitting on their boards, and fashioning industry policies that affect them. The bureaucrats let the hybrids tap the capital market by giving them permission to list on China's stock exchanges ahead of other companies and allow them to take over other companies quickly—two crucial advantages. Haier, for example, grew rapidly by acquiring dozens of unprofitable collective and state-owned enterprises in the early 1990s. The bureaucrats also discreetly provide the hybrids with bank loans and licenses, particularly if they operate in industries that the government has opened up to foreign competition. The less protected the industry, the more competitive the hybrids have become, as the cases of Haier and Galanz in the home appliance industry demonstrate.

China's challenge to the rest of the global market has been difficult to track because it hasn't taken one predictable form, as Japan's or South Korea's did. Instead of a few, large, privately owned companies trying to make inroads in the international arena, four groups of Chinese companies are simultaneously tackling the global market. China's *national champions* are using their advantages as domestic leaders to build global brands. The country's *dedicated exporters* are attempting to enter foreign markets on the strength of their economies of scale. China's *competitive networks* have taken on world markets by bringing together small, specialized companies that operate in close proximity. And the *technology upstarts* are using innovations developed by China's government-owned research institutes to enter emerging sectors such as biotechnology. Each group, starting from a strong base of cost competitiveness, has found a way to make its presence felt outside China's borders.

National Champions

After competing for decades with global leaders selling products on their home turf, some Chinese companies decided to concentrate on developing and selling products not just in the domestic market but also overseas. These national champions, as we call them, have tested the waters confidently, because they have successfully kept their multinational rivals at bay at home. But overseas, they don't challenge their bigger opponents head-on. Instead, they scout for segments that the market leaders have vacated or aren't interested in serving because profit margins or volumes are low. They use their experience in adapting technologies and features to meet the price points of cost-conscious Chinese buyers to develop products for those segments. Not surprisingly, low manufacturing costs allow these national champions to turn a profit where their rivals can't.

Haier exemplifies this strategy. By the early 1990s, the company had battled Whirlpool, Electrolux, Siemens, and Matsushita to become the leader in China's market for home appliances. The $8.6 billion company manufactures 250 types of refrigerators, air conditioners, dishwashers, and ovens. When it entered the U.S. refrigerator market in 1994, Haier sidestepped market leaders like GE and Whirlpool. For five years, it focused on selling only compact refrigerators—units smaller than 180 liters—that could be used as minibars in hotel rooms or that students could squeeze into dorm rooms. The incumbent leaders had dismissed these market segments as peripheral, but they proved to be quite profitable for Haier, which last year had about half of the minifridge market.

The company's second strategic foray was equally cautious: In 1997, Haier entered the market for "wine coolers"—refrigerated units for storing bottles of wine—and captured 60% of that specialized segment last year. In 2000, Haier set up a design center in Los Angeles and a manufacturing facility in Camden, South Carolina, to expand the range of products it sold and to bypass the nontariff barriers imposed by the United States on imports of appliances. Haier has persuaded nine of the ten largest retail chains in the United States to carry its products, and the company has won several U.S. government contracts.

Haier's customers didn't demand groundbreaking innovations or state-of-the-art technologies; they only wanted products that were reliable, cheap, and designed to meet their basic needs. Like Haier, many Chinese companies can deliver such products in both low- and high-tech industries. That allows them to surprise their rivals who are more worried about disruptive technologies and breakthrough innovations. For instance, no one took much notice when the $2.7 billion Huawei overtook Shanghai Bell (an Alcatel joint venture) to become a dominant supplier of digital switches and routers in China. Market leaders Cisco, Nortel, and even Alcatel attributed Huawei's success to the peculiarities of the Chinese telecommunications market. They didn't feel threatened because they believed their high-end networking products were superior to Huawei's. So you can imagine how shocked they were when Huawei entered the low end of the international market with routers that were 40% cheaper than the competitors'. By 2002, Huawei had 3% of the world market for routers, and one Wall Street analyst was recently quoted in *Forbes* as saying that Huawei is "the biggest reason I know to sell Cisco stock."

Despite the advances they've made, China's national champions have found it difficult to leverage their strengths in some highly segmented markets because they lack a deep enough understanding of local tastes and customer habits—for example, in the markets for cosmetics and regional foods. Moreover, these companies haven't invested heavily in new product development or customization. Part of the problem is that not all of them use proprietary technologies. Chinese DVD manufacturers, for instance, depend on Japanese and European companies for certain component technologies. Still, China's national champions are learning to overcome these deficiencies, employing the same techniques they've used before to fight their global rivals in the domestic market, including increased investment in R&D and novel marketing campaigns. (See "National Brands to Watch" for more information.)

National Brands to Watch

Company and Revenues (2002)	Products	Export Revenues as a Percentage of Total Sales Revenues (2002)	Share of the Global Market (2002)
Haier Group $8.6 billion	Home appliances such as refrigerators, air conditioners, microwaves, and washing machines	11.5%	About 50% of the U.S. market for small refrigerators; 60% of the U.S. market for wine coolers
Huawei Technologies $2.7 billion	Switches and routers for optical, mobile, broadband, and local-area networks	20%	3% of the market for routers
Legend Group $2.6 billion	PCs, notebook computers, motherboards, handheld devices, servers, and mobile phones	N/A	20% of the market for motherboards
Sichuan Changhong Electric $153 million	Color and rear-projection TVs, air conditioners, DVD and MP3 players, and batteries	44%	10% of the U.S. market for rear-projection TVs
Wanxiang Group $1.4 billion	Automotive components and systems, and aquaculture and agriculture products	17.8%	N/A

Dedicated Exporters

Despite the pull of the domestic market, some Chinese companies set their sights squarely on the external market when the government opened the economy. These dedicated exporters were probably motivated by the prospect of reaping global economies of scale or the knowledge that competition in their businesses was inherently global. Some of them attacked the overseas market from the start; others, which were subcontractors to big international players, had to think small at first to ensure that they didn't jeopardize their supplier relationships.

Not surprisingly, China's dedicated exporters first broke into mass markets, where they enjoyed an edge over rivals because of their low production costs. Take the case of Guangzhou-based Pearl River Piano, which set up one of the world's largest piano-manufacturing facilities in 1992. Even as the $88 million company established its reputation as a reliable supplier of pianos in the local market, it also scouted for a beachhead in the United States. By 1999, Pearl River had concluded there was demand in North America for a high-quality, inexpensive, entry-level piano—a gap it could easily fill as one of the world's cheapest piano producers. The next year, the company sent a four-member team to sign up distributors to help build the brand and launch the product in the United States. Despite the recession, the Chinese company increased its share of the U.S. market from 5% in 2001 to 10% in 2002. Not only is Pearl River investing more in its brands, it is also building a design center in Germany as a prelude to a European launch.

China's dedicated exporters don't confine themselves to the volume game. As they develop expertise with crucial technologies, they migrate to specialized, high-value segments. They aren't shy about striking partnerships or acquiring rivals to move up the value chain. For instance, CIMC set up six plants along China's coast in the 1990s to manufacture shipping containers. Because of its cost structure and the boom in China's trade, the $1 billion company became the world's largest producer of standard freight containers by 1996. In 1997, CIMC bought Hyundai's container-making operations in China, primarily for Hyundai's refrigerated-container-manufacturing technology. Over the next five years, CIMC captured half the world market for refrigerated containers. By 2002, the Chinese company had developed the ability to design and manufacture a full range of refrigerated containers—for air, sea, road, and rail—and is still the only company in the industry to have done so.

The speed at which China's dedicated exporters are able to master important technologies and component designs is impressive. The $1 billion Galanz, for example, started out in 1997 producing microwave ovens for the local market and for a few Japanese and European companies. Two years later, the company produced 200,000 units, and in 2002, it manufactured 15 million microwave ovens for more than 200 brands worldwide. As it moved up the learning curve, Galanz invested $100 million in R&D and bagged 600 patents in microwave-related technologies. Many customers depend on the company not only for manufacturing capacity but also for technological innovations and product-engineering skills. Having mastered microwave technology, Galanz launched its own brands in Europe, where it held a 40% share of the market last year. Likewise, it is only a matter of time before Chinese suppliers like Midea and BYD Battery, two of the world's largest manufacturers of fans and rechargeable batteries, respectively, start building their brands.

China's dedicated exporters have thrived in industries where competition centers on manufacturing excellence, low costs, and high economies of scale. However, these companies are at a disadvantage when product choice or service is critical for success. In such markets, the lack of experience in global marketing and service delivery has proved to be a handicap for these companies. But the exporters are trying to acquire the capacity to enter specialized segments by outsourcing brand-building skills and by striking alliances with distributors outside the country rather than going it alone. (See "Exporters to Monitor" for more information.)

Competitive Networks

In the city of Wenzhou (population about 7 million) in Zhejiang province, south of Shanghai, the manufacture of cigarette lighters began in the mid-1980s, when locals brought them back from Japan as gifts. The enterprising Wenzhouers broke the gadgets down into components and learned to produce replicas. By 1990, more than 3,000 families in the city were making lighters. The intense competition among them soon forced a shakeout. The smaller family businesses switched to making components for the lighters, and the larger companies focused on assembling them. That's how the Wenzhou network, about 700 private companies that operate as a single unofficial entity, came into being. This specialization drove down their manufacturing costs; the cost of an igniter, for instance, fell from $1 in 1990 to 25 cents in 1999. That allowed the Wenzhou network to enter the international market. It sold based on price at first but

Exporters to Monitor

Company and Revenues (2002)	Products	Export revenues as a Percentage of Total Sales Revenues (2002)	Share of the Global Market (2002)
BYD Battery $275 million	Rechargeable batteries	80%	39% of the market for batteries in electric tools; 72% of the market for batteries in mobile phones; 38% of the market for batteries in toys
China International Marine Containers $1 billion	Transportation equipment, including containers, trailers, and airport support equipment	95%	46% of the market for standard freight containers; 50% of the market for refrigerated containers
Galanz $1 billion	Home appliances, including microwaves, air conditioners, electric rice cookers, and electric fans	30%	40% of Europe's microwave oven market
Pearl River Piano $88 million	Wind, string, and percussion instruments, including pianos and guitars	22%	10% of the U.S. piano market
Shanghai Zhenhua Port Machinery $370 million	Cranes and other equipment for handling bulk materials	90%	35% of the market for harbor cranes

earned higher margins as it learned to produce new designs faster. Last year, the Wenzhou network manufactured 750 million lighters and enjoyed a 70% share of the world market. Because of the Wenzhou network's dominance, most of the Japanese and South Korean companies that used to control the lighter business are gone.

There are a number of competitive networks, or clusters, in China, each made up of hundreds of small entrepreneurial companies (and their families) located in one geographical area and operating as a cohesive, interdependent entity. Since the networks have few, if any, bureaucratic systems and little, if any, corporate overhead, they are highly flexible, low-cost producers. They thrive in markets that require quick responses to changes in demand. Foreign executives usually ignore them because the networks don't conform to the conventional notion of a globally competitive organization. But their power shouldn't be underestimated. China's networks have taken the markets for watches, socks, shoes, toys, pens, and Christmas decorations by storm, capturing market shares of as much as 50% in some of these industries. Indeed, in these markets, the "made in China" tag has itself become a powerful brand among distributors and retailers.

Many of China's networks operate in industries where changes in style affect demand. They've hired fashion houses in Asia and Europe to fill the gaps in their knowledge and to help them anticipate trends. For instance, a 1,000-unit network in Shengzhou, a rural county that is also in Zhejiang province, produces 250 million neckties a year. The network is in a mountainous area where the average per capita income is less than $1,000 per year, so its manufacturing costs are low. Over the last two years, the network has invested $40 million to improve the technology it uses and has hired several experts from Europe to improve product design and quality. The network has also become a supplier to international fashion houses like Armani and Pierre Cardin. The Shengzhou network codesigns ties with the fashion houses—using collaboration software over the Internet—and turns the designs into products in just 24 hours. The network supplies the bulk of its products to European retailers. Its product quality and designer links have enabled it to challenge the Italian, French, and Spanish incumbents at the top end of the market.

It is not easy to get a network to coalesce out of a rabble of competing firms. At first, every family aspires to become an assembler of the final product—the link in the chain that is seen as most prestigious. Over time, however, companies realize they will be better off specializing in activities that allow them to play to their strengths. Local government in China often helps the process by offering incentives, licenses, and approvals in ways that encourage specialization and eliminate internal rivalry.

The weakness of China's networks is their inability to make the investments necessary to build brands. But just as Benetton successfully brought together several of Italy's small knitting firms, a few large Chinese companies are exploring the possibility of linking up with the networks to help them realize their full potential. (See "Networks on the Rise" for more information.)

Technology Upstarts

Many Western managers believe that high-tech businesses are immune to competition from Chinese

Networks on the Rise

Network Location	Products	Export Revenues (2002)	Share of the Chinese Market (2002)	Share of the Global Market (2002)
Chenghai and Shenzhen (Guangdong province)	Toys	$5.1 billion	N/A	26%
Shengzhou (Zhejiang province)	Neckties	$300 million	84%	20%
Shenzhen (Guangdong province)	Christmas decorations	$2.4 billion	N/A	N/A
Wenzhou (Zhejiang province)	Lighters	$71 million (2001)	95%	70%
Wenzhou (Zhejiang province); **Jinjiang** (Fujian province); **Dongguan** (Guangdong province)	Shoes	$10 billion	N/A	50%

companies. That's a dangerous misconception, especially when you consider that, among other things, gunpowder, paper, and the compass were all invented in China. Under the central-planning system, the Chinese government built a large infrastructure for basic scientific research and developed sophisticated military-related technologies. The research could be used only by the government or the military and wasn't commercially exploited for decades. That changed in 1984, when the government shook up the research community and forced state-owned laboratories to obtain most of their funding by commercializing the technologies they developed.

China's research institutes have spawned several companies to take their technologies to market. For example, Legend, China's biggest PC manufacturer, was set up in 1984 by a group of scientists who worked at China's Institute of Computing Technology. Other institutes have encouraged their scientists to turn into entrepreneurs. China's Institute of Biochemistry and Cell Biology, which is funded by the Chinese Academy of Sciences, in 1999 succeeded in generating a DNA array representing 8,000 human genes. The institute encouraged one of its scientists to use the research to develop a protein chip that would allow the diagnosis of several types of cancer through a single test. The scientist floated a company, Shanghai HealthDigit, which used funds from commercial investors to develop the biochip, which was approved by China's FDA in 2001. Last year, the company sold 150,000 units of the chip—still the only one of its kind in the world—to 200 hospitals across Asia.

Several Chinese companies have also used state-of-the-art technologies created in government laboratories to develop products for the world market. Beijing

Founder Electronics, which dominates the market for electronic systems that publish Chinese characters, has drawn on several technologies produced by state-funded research projects at Beijing University, for example. That has enabled the $1.7 billion company to become a challenger in the high-resolution electronic publishing systems market.

Companies are able to buy technologies relatively inexpensively because the Chinese government usually has underwritten most of the costs. The state set up a string of institutes in the mid-1990s for biotechnology and broadband mobile telephony research, and they spawned several start-ups. Datang Microelectronics, for example, has drawn on research done by China's Telecommunication Research Institute to become a major global player in the design and manufacture of integrated chip sets.

China's technology upstarts are enlisting support from the large numbers of people who left the country in the late 1970s to study overseas. In fact, it isn't unusual to find start-ups in China with a local CEO, a CTO groomed in Silicon Valley, and a CFO from Hong Kong or Taiwan. For instance, the Hangzhou-based business-to-business portal, Alibaba.com, boasts a CEO from China, a COO from Hong Kong, a CTO from the United States, and a CFO from Taiwan—all of Chinese descent. (See "High-Tech Start-Ups" for more information.)

THE COMPANIES DISCUSSED in this article are the forerunners of the globally competitive organizations that will emerge from China in the future. The country's new leaders President Hu Jintao and Premier Wen Jiabao believe that building multinationals will help China

High-tech Start-ups

Company and Location	Year Founded	Technology Source	Technology or Product	Global Revenues (2002)
Beijing Yuande Bio Medical Beijing	1999	Beijing Medical University	Ultrasound tumor therapy device	N/A
Datang Microelectronics Beijing	1998	Telecommunication Research Institute	Integrated circuit design and manufacture	$36 million
Innova Superconductor Beijing	2000	Applied Superconductivity Research Center, Tsinghua University	Superconductors, and super-conductor wires	N/A
Shanghai HealthDigit Shanghai	2000	Institute of Biochemistry and Cell Biology, Chinese Academy of Sciences	Biochip for detecting cancers	$5.6 million
Tsinghua Solar Beijing	1989	Tsinghua University	Solar energy collection tech-nology	$365 million

Note: The four tables were compiled from published data and company interviews. Global market shares have been estimated by industry associations.

become an economic superpower and have started implementing policies that will spur the growth of more Chinese brands. For instance, former president Jiang Zemin announced in March 2001 a "going abroad" policy to encourage Chinese companies to invest overseas. While the Chinese government has been leery about providing subsidies and incentives to companies that want to be global players, it has started removing some of the roadblocks in their path, such as tedious project approval processes, stringent foreign-exchange controls, and a state monopoly over exports.

The Chinese government already supports 22 companies with global potential—six whose goal is to be among the 500 biggest companies in the world and 16 that want to build global brands. They get speedy government approvals for, say, foreign investments; a few subsidies like smaller social welfare burdens; and easy access to bank credit for working capital. The government has also publicly recognized the efforts of CEOs who have set out to build global brands, like Haier's Zhang Ruimin. Moreover, competition within China will become fiercer as the government implements its promise to the World Trade Organization to cut tariffs from an average of 24.6% in 2002 to 9.4% by 2005. At the same time, Chinese companies will find it easier to break into foreign markets because the European Union, Brazil, Mexico, and the United States will reduce tariffs and abolish quotas on Chinese imports. Indeed, China's hidden dragons could be your company's biggest rivals in the next five years.

Originally published in October 2003
Reprint R0310F

Short-Term Results

The Litmus Test for Success in China

RICK YAN

Executive Summary

DESPITE CONCERNS ABOUT the continuation of China's economic boom and the country's political future, multinationals are flocking to China. Why? Because China may soon be one of the world's most important economies. Companies that don't consider exploring this vast market may be overlooking a tremendous growth opportunity.

Investing in China now to build sustainable long-term positions is a credible strategy. Some companies, however, have taken the long-term argument too far. They tolerate poor short-term results in the mistaken belief that such results are a trade-off for future profitability. But underperformance in the short term is a good indicator that a company's strategy or practices may not measure up over the long run.

Drawing on the examples of multinationals already competing in China, the author finds that success is more a factor of managerial capability, critical mass scale, and product portfolio than it is length of stay. Although some early movers are market leaders, being number one requires more than longevity. Take Coca-Cola, for instance. To see it as a passive player that "waited it out" is to misunderstand the company's aggressive strategy: Coca-Cola planned carefully for success and executed a series of smart short-term moves to make it happen.

In the final analysis, players that want to be around over the long run had better make the right moves today. One mistake won't seal a company's fate, but organizations need to learn from their mistakes quickly and use their new knowledge to build winning strategies. Companies that fail to adapt to the fast-paced market will never enjoy long-term success in China.

CHINA HAS TRADITIONALLY bewitched multinational companies. They come and they invest. They invest despite nagging concerns about the continuation of China's economic boom, despite uncertainties about China's political future and its commitment to a market economy. Enchanted by the promise that it will be one of the world's most important economies by early next century, many multinationals are approaching China as a long-term strategic market, and they are investing large sums of money to help build sustainable long-term positions. This can be a rational strategy. Multinationals that do not consider exploring China's vast market with its emerging consumer base could be missing a tremendous growth opportunity. But some multinationals take the long-term argument too far.

Although making profits is a matter of necessity, even of urgency, at home, some multinationals are not making—and do not expect to make—money in China in the short term. Moreover, these companies tend to point to early entrants, such as Coca-Cola, to support their belief that you have to be around a long time to get results, that it is critical to stay on in order to reap the early-mover advantage. This is nonsense.

Underperformance in the short term is probably the best indicator we have that a company's current strategy or practices—or both—may be outdated and may not measure up over the long run. This is particularly true where no attractive opportunities exist in the market. (See "When You Should Consider Exiting the Market" at the end of this article.) True, Shanghai Volkswagen, Matsushita's TV tube factory, Charoen Pokphand's animal feed ventures, and Otis's elevator plant are all early entrants that are growing at double-digit rates. But Peugeot entered the Chinese market at the same time as Volkswagen, and it has lost tens of millions of dollars each year since 1995. Kraft entered China more than ten years ago, and all of its plants are now reported to be losing money.

Why are short-term results so crucial? Because in a turbulent market such as China's, sustainable long-term positions are necessarily built on a series of successful short-term moves. Short-term results can help build brand recognition, attract local talent, and secure support from the parent company. They can create a virtuous cycle.

By contrast, a vicious cycle is established when a multinational company sees no positive short-term results. Rather than revise the company's strategy, managers typically justify underperformance with the argument that China is a long-term market. That is usually a serious miscalculation. The hard truth is this: when no positive short-term results are seen, critical mass is not achieved, so the overhead cannot be spread over a reasonable volume. Therefore, the operations lose credibility back at the home office. As a rule, the China business is then scaled back in order to reduce short-term losses. The expatriate staff, for example, may be cut excessively even when the local Chinese staff is not ready to assume more responsibility. In general, market share falls, and the Chinese operations are second guessed: How far should we go? How hard should we push? When will we see results? How attainable are the long-term targets? Given these dynamics, players that want to be around over the long run had better be making the right moves today—or they'll be sitting on the sidelines before tomorrow's game even begins.

Does this mean that you've got to get it all right, all the time, every time? No. Everyone makes mistakes. But multinationals must learn from their mistakes—and learn fast. Long-term success is best achieved through measurable short-term results.

Coke Is It!

Multinationals often point to Coca-Cola's achievements in China as strong proof that endurance will eventually lead to success. But to understand Coca-Cola as a passive player that "waited it out" is to seriously misunderstand the company's strategy and management capability in China. Coca-Cola planned vigorously for success. Its position as market leader is founded on an extraordinary ability to react in a timely and accurate way to changing market dynamics. As a result, Coke led Pepsi right from the start, and Coca-Cola has been profitable for more than ten years in China. Pepsi-Cola, which entered China with its Shenzhen plant in 1982—just one year after

Coca-Cola—is still trying to break even. Today sales of
Coke are almost three times those of Pepsi. Coca-Cola
has 23 bottling plants in China, nearly double the number that Pepsi-Cola has. And three of Pepsi-Cola's plants
produce only local cola brands because the volume of
Pepsi didn't grow quickly enough to utilize the capacity.

What gave Coca-Cola its advantage? A closer look
shows that the company dominated the soft-drink
industry not by being an early mover but rather by making a series of brilliant short-term moves. When Coke
was first introduced in China, it was not well accepted by
Chinese consumers. For one thing, Coke looked and
tasted a bit like a Chinese herbal medicine. In addition,
most of the soft drinks in China at the time were orange
flavored and light colored. So from the beginning, Coca-
Cola invested in Sprite and Fanta as well as in Coke; in
the early 1980s, in fact, more Sprite than Coke was sold.

There are many reasons for Sprite's popularity. Most
Chinese women prefer Sprite to Coke, and many consumers mix Sprite with beer or red wine. As Coca-Cola
continued to invest in the Coke brand, and as consumer
acceptance improved in the 1990s, sales of Coke eventually exceeded those of Sprite. Today, the Coke-to-Sprite
volume ratio is four to three. In contrast, Pepsi-Cola has
been less successful with 7-Up: the Pepsi-to-7-Up ratio is
four to one.

Coca-Cola's long-term success has also involved taking as much control as possible of its joint ventures. In
the early 1980s, foreign investment in the Chinese beverage industry was highly restricted; Coca-Cola was forced
to form partnerships with government bodies. It chose
COFCO (China National Cereals, Oils and Foodstuffs
Import-Export Corporation), which monopolized the
food import-export business, and the Ministry of Light

Industry (recently restructured as the State Light Industry Bureau), which oversaw the development of the domestic food and beverage industries. Coca-Cola did not have equity majority, so it had only limited management control of the bottling joint ventures. In 1988, when regulation of bottling joint ventures was relaxed, the company moved quickly to acquire stakes from its partners to establish majority equity positions and to gain management control.

Coca-Cola didn't stop there. It shifted its entire partnering strategy at the same time by inviting three partners—Citic (China International Trust and Investment Corporation), Swire Pacific, and Kerry Group—into its new bottling joint ventures. Citic is a state-owned investment conglomerate formed by the directive of the late Deng Xiaoping. It has arguably the most Western style management approach and the most astonishing *guanxi*, or connections, in China. Swire Pacific is Coca-Cola's partner in Hong Kong. It is one of the leading trading *hongs* there and enjoys a good relationship with the Chinese government. Kerry Group is owned by the Malaysian tycoon Robert Kuok, who holds significant investments in China and has top-level access to Chinese leaders. With these strategic partnerships, Coca-Cola was actively positioning itself for the future.

Coca-Cola's foreign partners serve a number of the company's critical objectives. They share its investment risk in the bottling plants. In China, as in other parts of the world, Coca-Cola focuses its capital investment in the concentrate plant, thereby minimizing its share in the more capital-intensive bottling plants. At the same time, it is able to leverage the political influence of its partners to get government approval for new bottling plants. But most important, these new partners give

Coca-Cola management control through equity majority ownership of the joint ventures.

Pepsi-Cola, in contrast, did not seek equity majority and management control until 1993. As a result, four of its bottling plants remain cooperative joint ventures rather than equity joint ventures. There are considerable disadvantages to cooperative joint ventures. Because they are based on cooperative contracts, they restrict the foreign party's level of management control and complicate the process of making investment decisions. In short, when it comes to the Chinese market, Pepsi-Cola's lackluster performance shows how even an experienced marketer can miscalculate the critical factors for success.

Pepsi-Cola had not even begun to wrestle with the question of partnerships in the early 1990s, when Coca-Cola was already taking important strides toward investing in a direct distribution system. Coca-Cola's plan was simple: make Coke more readily available through a direct sales force. The consequences of this strategy were significant. The new distribution system allowed Coca-Cola to invest in opening new accounts, which increased coverage. The company was able to provide better service to retailers, perform merchandising and point of sale activities, motivate retailers, manage inventory levels, and increase profitability by capturing the wholesaler margin. Almost all of these activities would be considered elementary by Western standards, but they were entirely new to bottling partners and traditional wholesalers in China. So they gave Coca-Cola an edge. The result: with direct distribution in place, today 65% to 70% of Coke's sales are managed through its own sales force, compared with only 20% of Pepsi's. Coca-Cola is also able to cover more than 90% of urban areas, compared with Pepsi-Cola's 60%.

Those moves in themselves would have been enough to demonstrate Coca-Cola's mettle and determination to be the market leader, but the company nonetheless launched another offensive in the form of a bold investment policy. Although Coca-Cola has already invested $500 million in China, it recently announced that it will double its investments to $1 billion over the next five years. The implications for market share are significant. Today both Coca-Cola and Pepsi-Cola have bottling plants in major cities such as Beijing, Shanghai, Guangzhou, and Wuhan. Problems will emerge, however, as soon as the two competitors try to expand into smaller cities, where the volume potential will justify only one plant with sufficient scale to break even. The government has already announced that it will grant just one license in these cities. As a result, huge entry barriers will be established once a plant is built in a small city. Given Coca-Cola's profitability and leadership, the picture looks bleak for Pepsi-Cola. If its announced plans are realized, Coca-Cola will most likely continue to lead Pepsi-Cola in market share by a margin of three to one.

Coca-Cola's long-term success underscores why short-term results in volume growth and market-share leadership are absolutely essential. Its strategy allowed it to build sustainable advantages in the market by attracting better management talent and producing sufficient volume and profits to invest in a direct distribution system. This early success reinforced its commitment to the Chinese market. And it also deepened Coca-Cola's understanding of the market and Chinese employees, thereby facilitating the relationship-building process with the government. A virtuous cycle was set firmly in motion.

Patience and Longevity Are Not Enough

Early movers do not necessarily succeed. More important success factors include managerial capability, critical mass scale, and product portfolio. This is true in any market but perhaps more so in China, where local market knowledge is not always intuitive or obvious. Kraft, for example, was an early mover that could not sustain its initial success—in part because of an inappropriate product portfolio in a quick-paced market.

Kraft entered China more than ten years ago with its product Tang. Subsequently, the company built three additional plants for producing coffee, dairy products, and gum. Despite this expansion, Kraft's market position in all product categories today is weak. Sales of Tang, for instance, declined 25% in the last five years, eroded by many emerging substitutes, such as Jianlibao, a carbonated orange-flavored drink, and by numerous fruit juices. In coffee products, Kraft's Maxwell House has always fought an upward battle against Nestlé's Nescafé. As for the sale of dairy products, cheese and yogurt are not part of the traditional Chinese diet. Kraft's competitors have gained market share by offering Chinese consumers products that are more suited to their tastes. Nestlé behaves much more like a Chinese food company. In addition to offering global brands such as Nescafé, Nespray, Milo, Kit Kat, and Polo, Nestlé has tailored several products to what the Chinese consumer wants and needs—instant noodles, seasonings for Chinese cuisine, mineral water, and a popular live-lactobacillus health drink. Unless consumer-goods companies can adapt in this way to build a more attractive portfolio of product categories, they are unlikely to be successful in China.

Product portfolio is not all that a multinational company must get right. The operating paradigm it follows in its home country should be reevaluated for its effectiveness in the local environment. For instance, given the low labor costs and the weak wholesaler capabilities in China, it often makes sense to have a direct sales force service key accounts instead of relying solely on wholesalers for distribution. Moreover, for many consumer products, often as many as half the consumers have not decided which brand they will buy when they enter a retail store. As a result, in-store promotions tend to be more effective than advertising.

In addition to reconsidering the best approach to distribution and marketing, a company might also have to adjust its product's packaging. Consider, for example, the performances of Budweiser and Miller in the premium beer market.

Budweiser was launched in China in 1995. By 1997, it had leapfrogged to the number one position in the extremely competitive premium segment. Demand for Budweiser far exceeded capacity. Anheuser-Busch—the U.S. company that owns Budweiser—decided to double its capacity in China. It rationed beer to wholesalers until new capacity came on stream in the summer of 1998.

Anheuser-Busch achieved this success because it made a point of knowing its market. Before entering China, it had taken the time to study customers and had learned that in China, the characteristics of premium beer are very different from those in the United States. In China, some 70% of premium beer is consumed in restaurants and bars, only 30% at home. Chinese consumers choose cheap popular beer when drinking with their families, but when they eat out with friends, they order premium-priced beer in order to save face. In restaurants, moreover, beer drinkers like to share large bottles as a sign of courtesy and friendship. Because of low labor costs and subsidized energy rates, glass bottles in China are only half the price they are in the United States. Cans cost twice as much there because China can't produce aluminum sheets, and can makers have to source them overseas, paying a high import duty.

Predictably, the most popular packaging for premium beer is the 22-ounce bottle. In packaging its product, Anheuser-Busch was quick to accommodate the needs and wishes of Chinese consumers; the reaction in the Chinese market was immediate and positive. By contrast, Miller—the number two beer in the United States after Budweiser—was launched in China in 1992, almost three years before Budweiser. At the time, Miller was available only in cans. Not surprisingly, it did not sell well and was discontinued in 1994. Miller Brewing reintroduced its beer in cans and large bottles in 1996. Due to fierce competition and the lack of investment support, the company struggled and pulled out of the market after only a few months. Currently, Miller has no local production in China and has only a tiny share of the niche import-beer segment. Clearly, early presence in the market provided no defensible advantage.

In fact, early movers are sometimes at a disadvantage. Diving in and treading water can be just as expensive as getting in too late. Consider the courier industry. In China, the courier market is highly regulated. When FedEx, UPS, TNT, and DHL first entered the market, they were all required to work with the same Chinese company, Sinotrans, as their exclusive agent. Although these players were accustomed to competing fiercely on a global scale, their restriction to the same agent in China stifled the level of differentiation between companies.

In the late 1980s, the government allowed Sinotrans to enter into equity joint ventures. Most players quickly moved to form fifty-fifty joint ventures; only FedEx held back. It adopted a two-pronged strategy that forced it to stick to the old agent arrangement but also enabled it to leverage its lobbying power to push China to relax the regulatory environment. The strategy paid off. FedEx has managed to sever its relationship with Sinotrans and pick a new agent. It has also secured landing rights in Beijing and Shanghai through its acquisition of Evergreen, an established cargo airline. FedEx has negotiated the "fifth freedom" landing right in Japan, so it can load cargo there during stopovers for its flights to China. Finally, after FedEx chairman Fred Smith met with Chinese President Jiang Zemin, FedEx obtained the right to fly to Shenzhen.

If FedEx had followed the competition, it could not have adopted and implemented the same frontal strategy that it used, to great effect, in the United States in the 1970s and in Europe in the 1980s. Specifically, a fifty-fifty joint venture with Sinotrans would have prevented FedEx from playing the lobbying card so hard. It would have been significantly more complicated for FedEx to secure the rights to fly planes to Beijing, Shanghai, and Shenzhen, and it could not have made aggressive investments in its service network and marketing. (Under the fifty-fifty arrangement, the Chinese partner has to agree on—and cofund—those investments.) If the regulatory environment opens up still further and China joins the World Trade Organization, FedEx will be better positioned than its competitors to set up its own operations with full control and an extensive ground delivery network.

Paradoxically, although FedEx's competitors entered into a seemingly attractive deal, they ended up creating difficulties for themselves when market conditions changed. FedEx was the only company bold enough to wait, gambling that a joint venture could be a costly undertaking from which it would be difficult to extricate itself. Early-mover disadvantage can be expensive.

Short-Term Success Is Not a Pipe Dream

Traditional wisdom says that it takes a long time to make money in China, but a hopeful note can be sounded. A survey of the top 200 joint ventures in China reveals that they are growing at an average compound annual growth rate of 38% at an 8% after-tax margin. Moreover, individual examples of short-term success are impressive. For instance, Ericsson—the Swedish telecom company—acquired 40% of the cellular handset market, worth $4 billion, in only three years. Kodak gained a 15% share of the $500 million film market in less than two years. Tingyi built a $500 million instant-noodle business from nothing in just four years; its average operating margin over that period was more than 20%.

Many of these successes can be attributed to recent moves these companies have made, not to how long they have been in China. The examples of Ericsson, Kodak, and Tingyi show how companies can plan for success by making smart short-term moves, thereby helping to establish new rules for the game. Their successes are also founded on their continuous learning in the market and their ability to react correctly to changing dynamics. Performance is driven by an adaptive strategy that can be implemented rapidly. In this respect, recent developments in the cellular handset market are particularly instructive.

Ericsson was an upstart in the market, and it beat its competition through an imaginative and enterprising consumer-marketing approach. Using a flashy advertising campaign, the company turned cellular handsets into fashion accessories. As a result of its revision of the rules of the game, Ericsson poached market share from Motorola, the early entrant in the paging and cellular handset markets. Although Motorola once commanded a monopoly position, its early successes did not help it sustain its lead. Ericsson was able to take advantage of fundamental shifts in the demographics of cellular handset buyers and the transition from analog to digital systems. And in the process, it vividly demonstrated the limited advantage of the early-mover position.

Ericsson's first hit in the Chinese market was the model 377 handset, which was somewhat smaller than competitors' offerings and appealed to female consumers. Given the extensive distribution and service network already set up by established competitors, Ericsson decided to focus on advertising. After a series of brand image and product benefit ads, the company signed up a famous Chinese actress, Gong Li, for a series of lifestyle ads, which proved to be extremely appealing to women. Sales continued to explode despite competitors' launches of similarly sized products. Learning from its initial success with the celebrity ad, Ericsson launched an even larger advertising campaign with another actress, Maggie Cheung. This campaign was so popular among those surveyed that it was hailed as the best ad in China in 1997. Ericsson then introduced a series of color phones to reinforce its position with trendy women. Impressively, by 1997—less than three years after it first deployed its new marketing strategy—Ericsson had captured around 40% of the handset market in China.

Kodak is another player that managed to steal the spotlight. Before the widespread establishment of minilabs for film developing, Chinese consumers sent their rolls of film to large photo labs for processing. Most of the photo labs used domestic equipment, paper, and chemicals; the high-quality advantage of foreign films could not truly be realized. It was Fuji—working with its distributor for Hong Kong and China—that started the minilab concept in China.

In the early 1990s, Fuji led the photo film market with a 60% market share. Due to the limited financing capability of its distributor, however, Fuji could not invest sufficiently in minilabs to dominate the market. Kodak jumped in and franchised its own network of more than 3,000 Kodak Express minilabs—roughly 50% more than Fuji had. Because Chinese consumers believe that Kodak films work better with Kodak equipment, paper, and supplies—and Fuji films with Fuji supplies—the wide network of Kodak minilabs drove up sales of Kodak film. Kodak's market share shot up by more than 15% in less than two years; earnings grew by more than 40% per year. Recently, Kodak committed to investing $1 billion in three local Chinese film companies. This will almost certainly provide Kodak with a quantum leap in the world's third largest film market, where Kodak already holds a 32% share of the market compared with Fuji's 35%.

Tingyi, the small Taiwanese food company that markets noodles, also muscled its way into the Chinese market, showing remarkable enterprise and persistence along the way. Tingyi's story is typical of the new winning strategy in China: strike while the iron is hot.

In the late 1980s, China's travel industry exploded when midlevel managers, students, and elderly people began to travel both for business and for fun. Airports and train and bus stations were jammed with travelers.

The transportation infrastructure was stretched to the limit, and there were no catering services in place to feed hungry travelers. Even now, restaurants can be found only in airports and in some large train stations; most of them are state run and are open less than six hours a day. Enter Tingyi.

Tingyi's success does not derive from having invented anything new but from staying ahead of the market. Consider instant noodles, which are hardly a new invention in China. The company's leading competitor—the mighty market leader in Taiwan, President Enterprises—already sold noodles wrapped in plastic. But it took Tingyi to recognize the real opportunity. It sold no-preparation-needed noodles in Styrofoam bowls. Plastic utensils and packaged seasonings were also included because hot water is the only resource widely available in public transport stations. The Styrofoam bowl concept was not new: a Japanese product called Cup Noodles had been around for much longer than Tingyi's product. But Cup Noodles was too small for famished travelers and—because it is imported from Japan—too expensive. Tingyi found a niche and exploited it. The company then maintained market leadership through innovations such as new seasonings and continual distribution expansion.

The moral is unambiguous: companies can make money quickly in China. As noted earlier with Coca-Cola, such success is not only feasible, it is crucial. The Chinese economy is changing very fast. It is experiencing high single-digit economic growth, the transition from central planning to a market economy, integration with the world trade systems, indigenous and imposed deregulation, the emergence of collective and private enterprises at the expense of state-owned enterprises, and so on. All these factors are dramatically altering the competitive landscape in many industries. The Chinese market is in such tumult that it is constantly challenging the positions of incumbents and creating fresh opportunities for innovative competitors that know how to change the rules of the game. It is fundamentally unsound to tolerate poor short-term results in the mistaken belief that they are an investment in the future. On the contrary, short-term success is critical both to generate profits for investments and to discourage competitors.

Smart Companies Learn and Adapt

The kind of success that Ericsson, Kodak, and Tingyi have achieved in the short term demands continuous learning and adaptability in order to manage the vastness of the market and the rapid rate of change. This is difficult in an environment like China, where Western managers face exceptional language and cultural differences, and doubly difficult because consumer demographics and tastes are constantly changing. Kraft's Tang was successful at the start, but carbonated drinks and fruit juices were quickly substituted for it. Motorola was very successful with male consumers, but Ericsson took advantage of the demographic shift in the cellular handset market toward women. As Ericsson's success dramatically shows, in an emerging market, effective learning is essential.

Consider Peugeot. Although Peugeot and Volkswagen entered the Chinese automobile market at roughly the same time, their performances have differed dramatically. Volkswagen's revenues have grown at a compound annual rate of 77% since 1985. Sales exceeded $2 billion

by 1995. Today Volkswagen has expanded its capacity to
300,000 cars; the company produces close to 200,000 cars
per year. It enjoys more than a 50% share of the passen-
ger car market and earns a double-digit after-tax profit.
By contrast, Peugeot has built a 90,000-car capacity and
sold only 2,000 cars in 1996. The company has lost tens
of millions of dollars annually since 1995.

Peugeot's poor performance appears to be caused by
its repeated inability to learn in and adapt to a rapidly
changing environment. As Volkswagen's success
demonstrates, the Chinese automotive industry is
attractive, and Peugeot began its operations in China
with plenty of advantages. Its joint venture was set up
in the wealthy south, which has a more entrepreneurial
culture because of its proximity to Hong Kong and
because of the early promotion of the reform policies of
the late Deng Xiaoping. By contrast, Volkswagen's joint
venture was established in the more conservative
Shanghai region. Until the mid-1990s, Shanghai's economy was dominated by loss-making state-owned enterprises, and the city was not allowed to implement
aggressive reform policies.

Yet Peugeot was not able to exploit its advantageous
position in the south and did not learn how to succeed
with commercial customers. In the 1980s, automobile
industry experts predicted that growth would be driven
by consumer wealth and consumer demand. But the
market in China remained commercial. Even now, the
vast majority of Chinese consumers cannot afford to own
cars—more than 70% of the cars in China are purchased
by commercial companies. Volkswagen was quick to
adjust its assumptions and operating paradigms; Peugeot was not.

To serve the commercial market, Volkswagen built an aggressive distributor network and sales force. The company recognized that commercial buyers were less price sensitive than other consumers given that they needed—and were willing to pay for—high-quality after-sales servicing. Volkswagen was able to push volume through its distributors and achieve critical mass. This growing volume allowed Volkswagen to realize considerable scale economies, thereby allowing it to drive down prices. Because Peugeot never managed to develop an effective approach for commercial buyers, it never generated the prices and profits needed to motivate distributors. Without this high channel profit, it was unable to attract capable and aggressive distributors and could not develop a reasonable service network.

Peugeot also failed to learn other important lessons. An understanding of the development of downstream industries, for example, was crucial in identifying and promoting potential demand. Volkswagen's partner lobbied the government to support the establishment of taxi companies in Shanghai. Although consumers could not afford to buy private cars, their demand for taxi services supported the growth of taxi companies, which did buy cars—from Volkswagen. Peugeot did not follow a similar strategy. The company was unable to secure a dominant position in its home province in China. Hence, it never achieved critical mass and competitive cost position to grow its operations to a national scale. Losses piled up, and after a 12-year stay in China, Peugeot exited the market.

By contrast, successful companies learned to capitalize on the conditions of the Chinese market. When Ericsson first introduced the lifestyle ads, it received mixed responses from various consumer segments. Older men thought the ad was frivolous, and some even switched their televisions to other channels. The ad elicited positive responses from female audiences, however, and sales of cellular handsets soared. Encouraged by this initial success, Ericsson invested more money to develop the Maggie Cheung ad series. Learning brought further changes and successes. For its part, Kodak learned from Fuji that minilabs were an effective tool for gaining market share. Knowing that Fuji's investment capability was limited because of its distributor's restricted finances, Kodak outspent its competition. The results were outstanding. Similarly, Tingyi learned from its initial successes in product development and distribution. The company continued to invest in new product developments that cracked the code for what Chinese consumers need and want. These companies all learned from their successes; they were able to reinvest and replicate the process. Such short-term results are not only critical to fostering a virtuous cycle but also constitute the very basis for effective learning.

Making Money in China

Just as in any other market, a superior understanding of the changing environment and the successful implementation of shrewd strategies drive profitability in China. Early movers like Coca-Cola that continually adapt to China's shifting market will enjoy success. Early movers that are unable to learn from and change with the market, like Peugeot, will exit. Early movers that start strong but fail to stay abreast of shifts in the market, such as Motorola, will lose market share. Early movers that enter into unattractive arrangements too soon—recall the sit-

uation that most of the courier companies found themselves in—will experience early-mover disadvantages.
And late entrants, such as Ericsson, Kodak, and Tingyi,
will enjoy success, despite their late entries, if they know
how to make the right moves in an emerging market.

Short-term success is the best litmus test there is for
companies as they continue to monitor the external
environment, to influence the competitive landscape,
and to adapt their responses to opportunities and
threats. Any company operating in China today should
carefully analyze its situation, understand what differen-
tiates success from failure, and then formulate the best
course of action. Multinationals should continue coming
to China because the opportunities for growth and profit
are immense. But buying into the myth that the Chinese
market is so unique that companies need not be profitable in the short term will never do. That is like applying the medicine of witchcraft in a scientific age.

When You Should Consider Exiting the Market

WHEN SHORT-TERM RESULTS are poor, managers of
multinationals should ask themselves two questions: Are
there really attractive opportunities for this particular
industry here in China? and Do we have the right strategy for competing in that market? China is a large economy. And the rate of growth of many industries there
makes it a particularly enticing prospect. (See the exhibit
"Growth Opportunities in China.") Nevertheless, there
are not opportunities for everyone. When short-term
results don't materialize because of the lack of attractive

opportunities, the answer is to scale back or to exit the market. Here are four common reasons why market opportunities do not exist.

Special dynamics of an emerging market

After purchasing-parity adjustment, China is already the world's second largest economy behind the United States. However, there are 1.2 billion people in China, and the per capita GNP is roughly $3,000. Because only a tiny percentage of people can afford high-priced products, the market for branded luxury goods, such as a Sony Handycam, is very limited. Moreover, many of the wealthy Chinese consumers who can afford to buy luxury items travel abroad for business and for leisure. They tend to purchase brand-name luxury goods on these trips because they cost less—they avoid paying the high duty levied on products imported into China. In fact, it is estimated that more than half of the branded luxury goods purchased by mainland Chinese consumers are bought overseas. Therefore, to succeed in the Chinese market, the objective of a luxury-goods manufacturer should be to enhance brand image in order to appeal to the small percentage of wealthy consumers rather than to provide broad access to consumers.

No supporting infrastructure

The sales of certain products depend on the availability of supporting infrastructures. Truck and trailer sales, for example, depend on the availability of intercity highways. The development of electronic commerce depends on the size of the installed base of Internet subscribers. Even mundane products such as toilet cleaners require a supporting infrastructure. Some optimists

Growth Opportunities in China

Many companies are drawn to China because of the size of its economy and its high proportion—25%—of the world's population. Further growth in this emerging market is expected, thanks to continual economic development and increasing consumer wealth. Compare the compound annual growth rates of the beer, color TV, steel, and cement industries over a ten-year period in China and the United States. If the current rate of growth continues, the volume of many markets in China may soon surpass their U.S. counterparts.

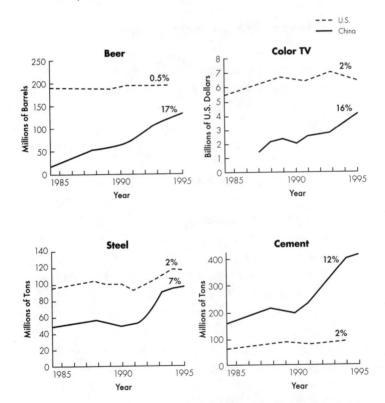

Sources: State Statistical Bureau (China), State Light Industry Bureau (China), Bureau of Labor Statistics (U.S.), Electronic Industries Association (U.S.).

believe that the potential market for toilet cleaners in China is a quarter of a billion households. Maybe one day. But for now, the number of installed Western-style toilets is only around 10 million households. Another 40 million toilets differ in shape from the Western style, while the remaining 200 million "toilets" are basically holes in the ground. Clearly, the potential for Western toilet cleaners is not what the 1.2 billion population figure might suggest but rather less than 5% of that number.

Overcapacity in the market

Chinese consumers are very curious about foreign cultures and new products. Like the Japanese, they want to keep up with their neighbors. This so-called herding phenomenon significantly accelerates product adoption and shortens the life cycle of products. Not surprisingly, the product adoption rate in China is three times that of the United States. (See the exhibit "The Influence of the Herding Impulse.")

Chinese companies also exhibit this herding behavior when they add capacity to take advantage of what they believe are attractive opportunities, causing likely overcapacity. Multinationals that time their market entry badly, or that simply act too slowly and miss the boat, will find themselves operating in an environment of industry overcapacity and depressing price trends as manufacturers try to sell their excess capacity. Under such circumstances, strong brands are essential in China if multinationals hope to maintain or grow market share and achieve profitability.

Restrictive regulations

The Chinese telecommunications market is huge. The number of new telephone lines added every year is more than the total number of telephone lines installed in Canada. But China does not have the technology to design and manufacture world-class switching products. Thus, selling these products to China's telecom companies is very attractive; Alcatel, AT&T, NEC, Nortel, and Siemens all profit in this market. But foreign participation as network operators—both fixed line and cellular—is carefully restricted, and the industry structure and dynamics are extremely unfavorable for foreign companies. Despite this environment, many foreign telecom giants were still keen to participate in the operator market. A

The Influence of the Herding Impulse

The so-called herding culture of Chinese consumers accelerates new-product adoption. The average penetration cycle (20%–60%) for consumer durables takes only 5 years in urban China compared to 15 years in the United States.

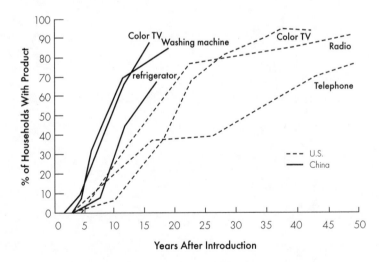

Note: China penetration for urban households only, a population of approximately 400 million.

Sources: *The Economist*, State Statistical Bureau. Data compiled in 1997.

number of vehicles were set up to tap the strong appetite of foreign players, but all of them turned out to be money losers. Staying in a market and losing money just doesn't make sense. If the industry structure is not attractive because of restrictive regulations, consider exiting.

Originally published in September–October 1998
Reprint 98511

Entering China

An Unconventional Approach

WILFRIED VANHONACKER

Executive Summary

CONVENTIONAL WISDOM HAS IT that the best way to do business in China is through an equity joint venture (EJV) with a well-connected Chinese partner. But pioneering companies are starting a trend toward a new way to enter that market: as a wholly foreign-owned enterprise, or WFOE.

Increasingly, says the author, joint ventures do not offer foreign companies what they need to succeed in China. For example, many companies want to do business nationally, but the prospects for finding a Chinese partner with national scope are poor. Moreover, there are often conflicting perceptions between partners about how to operate an EJV: Chinese companies, for example, typically have a more immediate interest in profits than foreign investors do.

By contrast, the author asserts, WFOEs are faster to set up and easier to manage; and they allow managers to expand operations more rapidly. That makes them the perfect solution, right? The answer is a qualified yes. First, foreign companies will still need sources of *guanxi*, or social and political connections. Second, managers must take steps to avoid trampling on China's cultural or economic sovereignty. Third and pehaps most important, foreign companies must be prepared to bring something of value to China—usually in the form of jobs or new technology that can help the country develop. Companies willing to make the effort, says the author, can reap the rewards of China's burgeoning marketplace.

If you're thinking about doing business in China, you've no doubt heard the conventional wisdom that the best—indeed, the *only*—way to enter China is through an equity joint venture (EJV) with a well-connected Chinese partner.

Listen again. China is changing, and so are the opportunities and challenges facing foreign companies that want to operate within its borders. Although EJVs are still necessary in some regulated sectors, and foreign investment is prohibited in others, there is a growing trend toward a new and possibly much more effective way of doing business in China—as a wholly foreign-owned enterprise, or WFOE. EJVs and WFOEs are substantially the same in terms of taxation and corporate liability. They also operate under similar foreign-exchange rules and comparable import and export regulations for licensing, quotas, and duties. In fact, their only real *technical* differences are that WFOEs take less

time to establish than EJVs, are not required to have a
board of directors, and are prohibited in some sectors in
which EJVs are approved.

Government statistics on the number of WFOEs currently operating in China are dated and perhaps mislead-
ing because they do not discriminate between businesses
and holding companies. But drawing on my experience, I
would characterize the movement toward WFOEs as
dramatic. In fact, I anticipate that half of all foreign
investments in China will be WFOEs by the year 2000.
For example, at the Suzhou-Singapore Industrial Park,
an industrial development area that the Chinese government calls a "showcase of the future," 94% of the 120
business projects approved so far are WFOEs, with an
average investment of $30 million per project.

Why are WFOEs taking hold in the current environment? The answer is *not* because of a change in China's
legal or regulatory codes. Instead, pioneering companies,
frustrated by the limitations and underperformance of
EJVs, have begun experimenting with WFOEs. Many of
those companies have met only minimal resistance from
the authorities. Chinese officials are proving far more
concerned about *what* outside investors bring to the
country—in terms of jobs, technology, and foreign
exchange—than *how* their deals are structured. At the
same time, foreign investors are finding that WFOEs,
because of the flexibility and managerial control they
deliver, make an excellent fit with China's competitive
situation today. The bottom line: WFOEs may well be the
win-win China strategy that businesspeople around the
world have been waiting for.

Consider the example of Johnson & Johnson. The company is famous in China for its successful pharmaceuticals EJV, one of the few examples of a well-functioning

partnership. But in 1992, seeking more control over sourcing and marketing, the company decided to launch its new oral-care, baby, and feminine-hygiene products venture as a WFOE. As expected, the new enterprise delivered the managerial control the company desired, and the results have been impressive. Since production began in 1994, the new venture's revenues have increased 40% to 50% per year. Indeed, the project is so successful that the company decided to make its latest investment—a business that will manufacture heart devices—a WFOE as well. And the company has indicated that in the future, all new investments in China will be WFOEs instead of EJVs, unless a Chinese partner offers a very significant contribution.

Contrast the Johnson & Johnson case with the experience of a U.S. household-products company that entered China in 1990 in an EJV with Shanghai Jahwa Corporation, China's largest cosmetics manufacturer. The U.S. company intended to capitalize on Jahwa's brand equity and distribution to push its own product line. Moreover, it hoped its Chinese partner would provide *guanxi*, the social and political connections required to make business run smoothly in China. Jahwa, meanwhile, hoped the U.S. company would upgrade the Chinese company's technology and increase its competitive capabilities both locally and abroad. These two companies shared the same bed, as the saying goes, but had different dreams. Their disputes over direction and resources paralyzed operations for three years. In 1993, Jahwa withdrew its top brands from the EJV and sold its share, leaving the U.S. partner scrambling for another local partner to salvage its investment and save face.

Indeed, the number of unhappy EJV stories such as this one are accumulating, and for similar reasons. To make matters worse, when EJV partners come to realize that their union is not working, Chinese culture makes EJVs hard to dissolve because relationships based on trust and confidence constitute the basic fabric of Chinese society. Same bed, different dreams—and divorce difficult! No wonder some companies have begun exploring the WFOE option.

China in Flux

China is a mystery to many foreign investors, and for good reason. The country is vast and varied, its culture and traditions are profoundly different from those of the West, and its social, governmental, and economic systems are particularly complex. Those obstacles alone would make a joint venture difficult. After all, joint ventures are notoriously hard to sustain even in the relatively stable environments of the United States and Europe. But today foreign investors must add several other ingredients to the mix when considering investment in China. Each ingredient makes an EJV less viable and suggests that a WFOE is the better alternative.

First, the marketplace in China is rapidly evolving, fragmenting, and becoming more competitive as more and more foreign companies set up operations there. Many new entrants are vying for first-mover advantage, and top-level players in some of the most promising industries—such as consumer packaged goods, infrastructure, construction, chemicals, pharmaceuticals, and electronics—are pursuing aggressive growth strategies with a focus on gaining market share. Some companies are willing to sustain losses in order to establish beachheads in China, be they in the form of manufacturing plants, distribution networks, or consumer awareness of their products. One result has been greatly expanded capacity—and in some cases overcapacity, which in turn has led to price wars and thinner operating margins.

Similarly, many foreign companies are attempting to expand nationally in China, an attractive but extremely difficult course. The distribution system in China is quite chaotic and is undergoing fundamental changes. For example, in Shanghai, the major retailers have recently restructured into three groups—the Number One Department Store group, the Hua Lian group, and the Friendship Store group—which together control the majority of retail space in that city of 13 million residents. These retail groups are also expanding nationally and trying to integrate the wholesale function, traditionally the weak link in China's distribution system, by buying directly from manufacturers.

At the same time, the traditional three-tier (national, provincial, local) distribution system in China is crumbling and giving way to various parallel channels that charge different fees and provide different services in every geographic area. The Finnish company Nokia, which sells cellular infrastructure and phones in China, recently identified at least six different distribution channels for its phones—with retail prices varying as much as 20% among them. These examples tell the same story: getting your product to market in China can be daunting. Expanding its scope can be even more so.

Exacerbating matters is China's industrial structure, a remnant of the country's planned economic system, which was in operation until 1979. That system created an enormously fragmented industrial environment. Companies were required either to make a narrow line of products or to operate in a narrow market niche. Today most companies retain that cramped scope. Very few have a national presence, and those that do have already been cherry-picked by early entrants, such as the Coca-Cola Company. In other words, the prospects for finding a Chinese EJV partner that brings national scope to the equation are poor.

China's planned economic system also left intact a rather rigid and hierarchical administrative structure. Every Chinese company belongs to and operates under some combination of local, provincial, and central government authority, each with its own agenda (and hence conflicting interpretations of rules and regulations). Borders between the authorities are sharply drawn, and many of them compete with one another for resources and regulatory protection. Thus if a company—your EJV partner, for instance—tries to do business outside its authorized territory, it is apt to run into trouble.

China's fixed-line telephone network, for example, is owned by and operated under the Ministry of Post and Telecommunication. Accordingly, the local operating companies belong administratively to the MPT. These local companies are all in the market for telephone switching equipment to upgrade and expand the network they operate. Shanghai Bell, Alcatel's large switching-equipment EJV in Shanghai, has a Chinese partner under the MPT. Its competitors, including NEC, Siemens, and AT&T, have partners under different ministries that are not involved with and have no regulatory authority over China's fixed-line network. It is no surprise that Shanghai Bell has an advantage selling its equipment to the local operating companies and commands more than a 50% market share.

Another aspect of this problem with market access: it is increasingly common that some Chinese partners are unable to find buyers for the EJV's output. In 1993,

Matsushita formed an EJV with Hualu Electronics Corporation, hoping to capitalize on Hualu's extensive domestic sales network. Originally, the plan was for Hualu to buy 80% of the joint venture's VCR components, which would then be installed in VCRs to be sold in China. However, since a new factory was opened in Dalian in 1994, most of the 45 production lines have been idle. Hualu is simply unable to absorb the joint venture's output. The bottom line of this story, and many like it, is that access to Chinese markets through an EJV is more limited than many foreign investors have hoped, and much more limited than most Chinese partners can deliver.

Access to Chinese markets is also being hindered by what was once thought to be the great door-opener: guanxi. Guanxi has long been touted as an invaluable asset to foreign investors. That assertion is still true. But more and more foreign companies are finding out that the scope of their Chinese partners' guanxi is limited, may take them in directions that are difficult to control, or may not be strategically useful. In addition, some companies are finding that guanxi may not be cost effective. The Danish company Novo Nordisk, while negotiating with two potential pharmaceuticals partners, realized it could get the approvals to do business as well as access to the bureaucracy in Beijing on its own. It ended up creating a $125 million biotechnology WFOE in Tianjin.

Conflicting Perceptions

Foreign investors today are faced with perceptions and expectations on the part of the Chinese that have changed in recent years. It is now commonly understood that most Chinese companies lack the experience to keep up with the speed and scope of change in the Chinese marketplace. They still approach sales and marketing largely with an order-taking mentality. And, not surprisingly, the whole concept and practice of free-market competition is alien to many Chinese. Many foreign companies have found it hard to keep their Chinese partners motivated for a fight, particularly when the partnership has attained a comfortable market position and level of operating profits. Consider Krohne, a German manufacturer of electromagnetic flow meters and a pioneer in China in 1985. It negotiated a minority equity stake in an EJV with a local partner in Shanghai. Within five years, the EJV was responsible for 60% of the installed flow meters in China and was enjoying a significant operating profit. That market position delighted the Chinese partner, which took it as a signal to relax, thereby causing enormous anxiety to Krohne's managers. They saw the company's success as an invitation to competitors and strongly urged their Chinese partner to step up investments to protect against the coming onslaught. Today, unable to come to an agreement about the best direction for the company, Krohne and its partner are in legal negotiations. Krohne, anxious for more managerial control, is hoping to increase its equity stake in the venture sharply.

Another area of conflicting perceptions and expectations concerns technology spillover. Indeed, this is perhaps the grayest of many gray areas of doing business in China. The desire for technology is one of the reasons China opened its markets in the first place. Foreign companies are expected to share what they know with emerging Chinese companies. But how much must they share? Chinese companies, naturally, want as much information as possible. Foreign investors, however, are reluctant to give away advanced, proprietary technology for fear that it will be copied—especially in light of China's spotty enforcement of intellectual property rights.

A third difference: it is now widely acknowledged that most Chinese companies seek profits on a much shorter time horizon than foreign investors. The interest in immediate profits most likely arises from concerns that China's experiment with capitalism may not last; such concerns may prove legitimate given China's swinging pendulum of government policy in recent times. Meanwhile, foreign companies entering China are sometimes willing to sustain losses for growth; more typically, they desire to reinvest their profits for further expansion.

Differences of opinion about profit taking have led to tensions in many EJVs. In fact, they ended up destroying the partnership formed in 1990 between a U.S. division of Saint Gobain, the diversified French group, and a Shanghai tool manufacturer. The Chinese partner considered the EJV a subsidiary and sought a quick profit from it. By contrast, the division of Saint Gobain viewed the EJV as a vehicle for strategic entry into China and spent $10 million to launch it. Not surprisingly, when market conditions hit a rough period soon after the partnership was formed and the joint venture began to lose money, the Chinese lost interest in the deal. (In fact, they neglected the project so completely that morale problems led to a rare strike by workers.) Saint Gobain's division meanwhile scrambled to keep the venture alive. Finally, after years of legal wrangling and central government involvement—and an additional $20 million of investment by the division of Saint Gobain—the company bought out its Chinese partner and turned the EJV into a WFOE in 1996, the first such conversion in Shanghai.

This case suggests the major advantages of WFOEs: They offer foreign investors increased flexibility and control. Within the constraints of the Chinese system, WFOEs allow managers to expand as quickly as they want and where they want—without the burden of an uncooperative partner. WFOEs also require foreign companies to set up, manage, and protect their own processes and procedures, which leads to more careful strategic, operational, and cost oversight. And they are faster to establish than EJVs; according to Chinese regulations, local authorities are required to respond to initial project proposals within 30 days. On the other hand, joint ventures can take years of negotiations to get up and running. In short, WFOEs deliver efficiency and effectiveness to an economic system in which both are in short supply.

But with this endorsement, some notes of caution must be sounded. First, a WFOE begs the question of guanxi. Can all companies follow the Novo Nordisk example and make the necessary political and social connections themselves? The answer is no. However, some foreign investors are relying more and more on agreements with Chinese agents to make liaisons on their behalf and to help procure land, materials, and services for them. These companies identify exactly which connections will help and who has them, and then engage the Chinese individuals, companies, or organizations with access to the decision-making authorities as "advisers" on short-term contracts.

Second, WFOEs do raise important questions about cultural and economic sovereignty. Naturally, the Chinese don't want foreign companies taking advantage of their country. A WFOE, if it is perceived as a foreign island, is particularly vulnerable to criticism. WFOE managers must recognize that concern and address it.

One way to do so is to localize production—that is, to buy as many parts and components as possible from local Chinese suppliers. Another way is to hire Chinese managers. Motorola's enterprise, for instance, employs only Chinese managers, very few of whom hold U.S. passports. Foreign companies can also be active in socially responsible projects, such as financing community movie theaters. Several foreign companies recently have shown their commitment to public safety by buying new cars for local police departments. WFOEs can also nurture local brands. Coca-Cola, for example, recently transferred the trademark of its new Tian Yu Di fruit drink to Tianjin Jinmei Beverage Company, a local producer of concentrate. This move was warmly received as an example of the company's sensitivity, in a country where being a piece of the puzzle is more valued than being a hammer on a nail. Indeed, if you behave like a hammer as a foreign investor in China, the nail will probably go into your own coffin!

Finally, it is important to note that WFOEs are not permitted in some industries, such as financial services and insurance. In general, they are prohibited in all service industries. But then again, the regulatory environment is still evolving, with more sectors opening up for foreign investment every year. The reason: China lacks the skills and resources to develop most industries on its own. I believe that if neither national security nor political and social stability are threatened, China will eventually grant investment access and increasingly approve WFOEs in the process.

WFOEs in Action

Today WFOEs operate in many areas where EJVs currently are approved: in manufacturing of machinery,

instruments, and equipment; in electronics and computers; in communications equipment; and in light industries such as textiles, foodstuffs, and packaging. In some
sectors, such as the automotive and telecommunications
industries, heavy regulations do apply, which usually
implies that EJVs are a safer bet. However, as Motorola
has proved in Tianjin and General Motors has proved in
Guangzhou, WFOEs are possible even in regulated
industries.

More important than what the rule books say are the
principles that underlie the rules. China wants and needs
its foreign investors to bring something of value to the
table. My experience has shown time and time again that
if they do, the form of investment is largely negotiable.
That's why WFOEs are just as feasible a way to enter the
market of the Middle Kingdom as EJVs.

So, what's of value?

Articles 5, 6, and 7 of China's Provisional Regulations
on the Guidelines of Foreign Investment, promulgated
on June 27, 1995, illustrate the government's concern not
just for national security, social welfare, and stability but
also for the environment and the proper use of the
nation's scarce arable land. They also show the government's interest in improving technology in the "priority"
sectors of agriculture, energy, transportation, and industrial raw materials. Likewise, several other technologies
are eagerly welcomed: those that improve product quality and raw materials efficiency (including the possibility
of recycling), provide products and materials in short
supply domestically, develop resources in the hinterland,
and have the potential for export.

A word about export. Some investors mistakenly
believe that there are higher export quotas for WFOEs
than EJVs. In reality, WFOEs probably do export more of
their production; that is, however, not a result of Chinese

regulations but an outcome of negotiations for the enterprise's approval. Unless the venture brings something
China wants, Chinese authorities will demand an export
quota of at least 50% from WFOEs as a kind of fee for not
working with a Chinese partner. Moreover, the authorities use this fee as a way to rationalize their approval
of the WFOE to higher government officials in the
bureaucracy.

Still, higher export quotas on WFOEs are not a major
obstacle. In fact, apart from the 70% export quota in
Article 11 required to secure approval of projects in
restricted industries, the rules and regulations on EJVs
and WFOEs do not specify what percentage of its output
a foreign company doing business in China needs to
export or how much it is allowed to sell domestically.
The EJV regulations stipulate only that "exports are
encouraged," which usually is interpreted to mean more
than 50%. Lower percentages can be negotiated when
the products are urgently needed domestically or when
they substitute for imported products and therefore save
China's hard currency. Similar principles hold for
WFOEs—although in practice, Chinese authorities have
tended to stick to a minimum 50% export quota. On the
other hand, I know of one WFOE recently approved in
Shanghai that has no export quota whatsoever because
of the enterprise's advanced technology.

A gradual process of liberalization in China—with
more and more sectors opening up for foreign direct
investment—is also helping the WFOE cause. Although
some sectors are likely to remain closed, local governments in particular are showing some give in their inter-
pretation and implementation of laws and regulations,
often with the objective of forcing Beijing's hand in relax-
ing or changing rules. For example, they have let some

WFOE retailers exist even though retailing is a sector closed to foreign investors. Such retailers have no import or export rights (for which State Council approval is needed). Some do not even have a retail license from the Ministry of Internal Trade, operating instead under a real estate management license provided by the local government. The foreign investors behind these operations prove that WFOEs are only a matter of trying—of pushing the limits and experimenting. This attitude may make many corporate attorneys squirm, but that is to be expected.

You may be wondering, If WFOEs make sense from a business and practical perspective, why even bother with an EJV? The answer is that picking between a WFOE and an EJV is not necessarily an either-or decision. Sometimes a Chinese partner does have a strong distribution network or operates in a restricted sector that is attractive to a foreign investor. In such situations, foreign companies can, for instance, surround their WFOE production operation with EJVs that market and sell their products in China. The Motorola operation in Tianjin does exactly that. Since 1993, Motorola has been laying the groundwork for the biggest U.S. manufacturing venture in China. Its $300-million-plus commitment to China focuses on pagers, simple integrated circuits, and cellular phones, and eventually will include automotive electronics. The production site in the Tianjin Economic Development Zone is a WFOE; marketing and sales of the products will be done through various EJVs with local partners.

Another possibility is to consider an EJV and a WFOE as a natural sequence: a foreign company gets initial entry and operates as part of an EJV for a fixed period; at the end of that time, it takes over the assets from the

Chinese partner and continues to run the operation as a WFOE. That is certainly an attractive alternative if the added value of the Chinese partner is significant but limited to the early stages of the venture. Some EJVs have integrated this option in the termination clause of the joint-venture contract.

Finally, it is possible to structure a WFOE under the legal umbrella of an EJV. In other words, the project would be an EJV as a legal entity but would be run and operated as a WFOE. Many foreign partners that have increased their equity stakes in existing ventures are going in that direction, in some cases turning their Chinese partner into a silent partner with a minority stake.

New Bed, New Dreams

In 1996, the Chinese leader Deng Xiaoping exhorted the Chinese people to embrace and accelerate economic reform so that China might avoid the fate of the Soviet Union and other former socialist republics now grappling with free-market systems. "I'm afraid the opportunity may be lost," Deng said. "If we do not seize it, it will slip away."

The same advice might well be given to foreign investors considering the WFOE option. For if EJVs are a case of same bed, different dreams, WFOEs offer a new arrangement for foreign investors and new hope for a more effective way to work and grow in a country with great promise.

But in any competitive market, turning dreams into reality is challenging. China's complexities redouble that challenge. However, foreign investors who can let go of the conventional wisdom that joint ventures are the only way to do business in China have a new way to take advantage of the Middle Kingdom's vast opportunities. For companies willing to accept the challenge, WFOEs are that way.

Originally published in March–April 1997
Reprint 97210

To Reach China's Consumers, Adapt to *Guo Qing*

RICK YAN

Executive Summary

WITH ONE-QUARTER OF THE world's population and consumer spending increasing by as much as 10% annually, China offers an opportunity that marketers of branded goods can't ignore. Foreign companies seeking to win a piece of this growing market must overcome nagging uncertainties about the country's stability. They must also understand *guo qing* ("Chinese characteristics" or "the special situation in China") in order to deliver a product with the value, quality, and convenience that will appeal to Chinese consumers.

For the Chinese, consumption is a novel pleasure. Having had very few choices for four decades, Chinese consumers are eager to see what's in the stores. They are especially curious about foreign goods, which are widely available now that regulatory restraints have been relaxed. Consumers' limited experience with modern marketing leads them to depend on reputable brands. In a wide range of goods surveyed, brands accounted for one-third to one-half of all consumer expressions of intent to purchase. Fancy displays and prime shelf space don't impress Chinese consumers; they have time to browse and will look for a product if they've heard of it. Marketers would do well to use the official media—television, radio, and newspapers—to advertise products: promotional gimmicks are alien to *guo qing*.

Given the fragmentation of most Chinese consumer markets, Western marketers should concentrate on 3 to 5 key cities and then build sales, distribution, and manufacturing capabilities over a wider area. Multinationals already operating in China should try to cover 15 to 20 key cities by the end of this century. The challenge for both new entrants and seasoned marketers is to continue adapting products and marketing practices to *guo qing*.

Tens of millions of people in China's Guangdong Province can afford a Western brand-name shampoo. For Procter & Gamble, this could represent the second largest market outside the United States. With 1.12 billion people—one-quarter of the world's population—and a rapidly expanding economy, China offers an opportunity that P&G and many other Western marketers of branded goods have decided they can no longer ignore.

But before these companies attempt to enter the Chinese market, they must overcome nagging uncertainties about the durability of China's economic boom; the government's ability to pacify peasants in the interior, who have not shared in this success; the international political fallout from the Tiananmen Square incident five years ago; and the inevitable struggle for power that will follow the death of China's leader, Deng Xiaoping. If any of those uncertainties give rise to xenophobia, Western companies could be ejected from China.

That these dark clouds on the horizon have not seriously dampened foreign investment in China is obvious from the figures: total foreign investment rose from U.S. $11 billion in 1992 to U.S. $111 billion in 1993. This enormous infusion of capital has helped make China the world's third largest economy (at U.S. $1.7 trillion, after purchasing-power-parity adjustments) after the United States and Japan.

For much of the Western world, consumption is a matter of routine, sometimes even a chore. Brand managers work hard to spark consumer interest in a television ad, a cents-off promotion, or a supermarket shelf. For the Chinese, however, consumption is a novel, pleasurable, and important part of the day. And in pursuing this pleasure, they do not hesitate to spend the bulk of their newfound "wealth"—more than 80% of their income. As a result, consumer spending is growing by 10% per year in urban households and 8% in agricultural households.

Guo Qing

Foreign companies seeking to win a piece of this growing market must adapt to *guo qing* (pronounced "gwor ching"), which means "national characteristics" or "a country's special circumstances." Understanding *guo qing* is crucial for brand marketers who want to deliver a product with the value, quality, and convenience that will appeal to Chinese consumers.

The term *guo qing* appeared in literature more than 2,000 years ago and was used in the 1920s to assess the socialist and communist ideas being introduced in China. In 1984, Deng Xiaoping issued a Communist Party directive that said, "Western cultures and ideas should be adopted only if they fit *guo qing*. Good ideas applicable in China should be promoted; corrupted and inapplicable ideas should be discarded."

The Chinese use the expression "does not meet China's *guo qing*" to criticize methods and ideas that they believe foreign governments or corporations may be imposing on them. Companies that have worked effectively with the Chinese win praise for their understanding of the concept. Most Western marketers venturing to China make a point of learning an appreciation of *guanxi* ("mutual trust" or "connection and relationships"), but that is not enough. Those who try to apply tried-and-true practices in product differentiation, shelf-space management, and other techniques that work well at home without taking *guo qing* into account will likely be disappointed.

A prime example of *guo qing* for Western marketers to consider is the government policy of limiting families to one child. The increasing burden of per capita pension costs and the growing number of unmarried males (a result of widespread abortions of female fetuses) will become very serious social issues in the next decade or so. The policy has already influenced family spending patterns in China: an estimated one-half of the premium goods that are purchased are bought for the only child— the "emperor" of the family. In particular, the high end of the baby- and children's-goods segments is growing quickly.

Another example of *guo qing* is the state ownership system, which has generated a lot of personal consumption, paid for by the liberal expense accounts of employees of ministries, the armed forces, schools, state-owned enterprises, and other organizations. This consumption is estimated at U.S. $16.6 billion, of which about one-quarter is unreported, and includes products such as autos, furniture, electrical appliances, and office supplies as well as health care and entertainment. Many foreign marketers have benefited. In 1993, for example, the Chinese imported some 100,000 autos; expense accounts paid for 99% of them. Such consumption is so well established that it has become part of *guo qing*.

Confucian philosophy pervades Chinese culture and is a central part of *guo qing*. Its characteristics include semi-isolation, self-sufficiency, and a strong bias toward obedience and against upward feedback and horizontal learning and sharing. When communicating, Westerners careful about honoring *guo qing* are advised to use official or senior channels. In advertising, for example, the accepted media for official pronouncements—newspapers, television, and radio—are the safest bets.

The Growth of the Chinese Market

During the past few years, China has relaxed regulatory restraints and opened up further to direct foreign investment. Foreign majority control and even 100% foreign ownership are allowed in most consumer-product markets. As long as a Western enterprise can balance its foreign exchange needs, the Chinese government does not limit imports of raw materials, impose export commitments on joint ventures, or restrict profit repatriation.

With the end of restrictive foreign exchange has come a blossoming of retail markets, the establishment of new distribution channels, and, most important, the availability of foreign goods in the local currency, the renminbi. Sales of foreign consumer goods have boomed. A container of Rejoice shampoo sells for 20 renminbi, which is 25% of an average weekly income; yet Rejoice is the leading shampoo in many major cities. One reason is that the Chinese have few alternatives for their disposable income since housing is subsidized and real estate prices put home ownership out of reach for most people.

In less prosperous times, Chinese consumers worked to acquire four status symbols: bicycles, watches, sewing machines, and radios. But wealth has spread, especially in the big cities. (See the graph, "New Wealth in Chinese Cities.") The Chinese are now saving money to purchase six *da jian*, or "big things": videocassette recorders, televisions, washing machines, cameras, refrigerators, and electric fans.

The 80% of income that hundreds of millions of Chinese consumers spend represents a considerable market, but it does not represent a big per capita expenditure. Relatively few Chinese can afford much: the average consumer spends less than U.S. $500 per year, even after purchasing-power-parity adjustment.

Still, the 10% annual growth rate of the urban economy is producing impressive sales results: high-end branded refrigerators, washing machines, and vacuum cleaners are finding buyers at 30% to 50% premiums over popular brands. In one of China's largest department stores (located in Guangdong), the ratio of premium-product to popular-product sales has shifted in two years from 30:70 to 50:50. In Shenzhen, a city near Hong Kong, the proportion is now 60:40.

The Chinese can afford such high levels of consumption because the government supplies, or at least subsidizes, life's essentials, including most staple foods. But because dining out is considered very prestigious and reflects the cultural value of social gatherings and the traditional importance of food, more than half of consumer spending in China is for food.

The government also heavily subsidizes other necessities, such as housing, clothing, and transportation, but as China moves to a market economy, such subsidies will likely be reduced and eventually eliminated. Along with food, then, these areas offer opportunities for Western marketers. For example, the cultural importance of the home and people's desire for durable furnishings are influencing shrewd brand marketers to stress the high quality of their household products.

Although most people work for the state, the movement to the private sector is growing. Marriages are often planned between one person who works for the

New Wealth in Chinese Cities

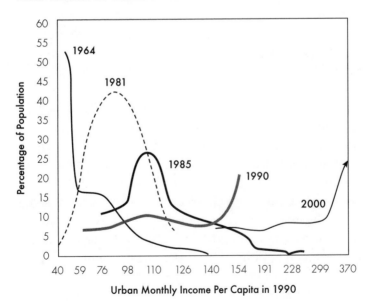

Source: Government Statistics, Beijing University.

government and another who works in the private sector; the former gets housing and other benefits, while the latter earns most of the income. The former also usually does the shopping. If you drop by a Beijing department store on any afternoon, you will find it packed with state workers (one reason for the low productivity of state employees).

Consumer Behavior

Many of the shoppers crowding Chinese stores are not serious buyers; they are "just looking." Having had very few choices for four decades, Chinese consumers are eager to see what's available, especially in foreign products. The Chinese saying "Never make a purchase until you have compared three shops" reflects *guo qing*. Chinese consumers have a lot of time to browse and, consequently, a disinclination for convenience or impulse buying. In Chinese cities, window-shopping and browsing are favorite weekend pastimes. The Beijing Lufthansa Shopping Center, a department store, has recorded 120,000 visitors in a single day.

Chinese consumers, tired of the low quality of their own goods, have a high regard for Western imports. Locally brewed Carlsberg beer and imported Carlsberg are sold side by side, but the import commands a 20% to 50% premium. Moreover, many Chinese brands that once carried premium prices are fast losing market share to locally made foreign brands. Even so, surveys show that consumers may end up rejecting a Western product that is made in China if its packaging does not look the same, or at least closely resemble, the packaging used in international markets.

Consumer behavior reflects *guo qing* in a variety of ways. For instance, the Chinese prefer propitious-sounding brand names, especially those that evoke powerful images. A kitchen-equipment manufacturer in Hangzhou tried several names for a product line, including Red Star, Treasure, and Prosperity, but could not find one that helped sales. Finally the maker tried Boss, and sales rose dramatically. A survey of retailers revealed that many customers asked for the Boss brand because the name implied good fortune and promised a robustness appropriate to the product that the other names did not.

Western brand managers also find that a symbolically significant name helps sell a product. When it was introduced in China in the 1920s, Coca-Cola sounded like "kou-ke-kou-la," which means "a thirsty mouth and a mouth of candle wax." The company changed the phonetic translation to "ke-kou-ke-le," which means "a joyful taste and happiness." Thirsty Chinese consumers responded in droves to the more felicitous "meaning."

The name Revlon is another big success in translation. Its meaning was linked to a famous poem describing the love between a Tang Dynasty king and one of the four most beautiful women in Chinese history. Revlon is translated as "lu-hua-nong," the last three characters in the second sentence of the poem, which mean "the fragrance of the flowers that are covered with morning dew."

Another aspect of Chinese culture that influences buyers' behavior is the reluctance to pioneer. (The Japanese are similar in this respect.) Typical Chinese consumers do not want to be among the first to try a new product, but the discomfort of being left behind may make them think that if the neighbors have tried it, they had better follow suit soon. Trials by early buyers thus soften the perceived risk for followers, who are then inclined to "pile on" in their haste to buy. Referral is the most powerful way of expanding trials to the first wave of consumers.

Strategies for Marketers

In the United States, marketing communication strategies usually hinge on an image or lifestyle association, or brand-equity maintenance. Manufacturers often assume that consumers have a basic knowledge of a product. Such strategies would be inappropriate for Chinese consumers. In China, the communication imperatives for products are: What is it? What is it called? What can it do? Where can a consumer find it? and (sometimes) How much does it cost? Simple, direct approaches work best, which keep product introduction costs low. Because of the enormous size of the markets, a trial alone can justify the investment in product development.

The novelty factor has worked well for many Western newcomers. P&G advertised Ariel laundry detergent on television for one month before making the product available in stores. By then, so much interest had built up that Ariel captured nearly 5% of the market in one month on the shelves.

After the curiosity factor fades, a company faces the challenge of sustaining volume. McDonald's successfully entered Hong Kong and later China at a premium of four to five times average eat-out costs. As the novelty wore off, McDonald's gradually reduced its premium in Hong Kong and China. Its positions in these markets continue to grow at a steady pace.

Kentucky Fried Chicken, however, took a different tack. The chain was a huge hit on its first entry into Hong Kong in the mid-1970s; long lines of customers formed every day. Although the novelty effect wore off in a little more than a year, KFC did not lower its high prices. Its business dried up, and the company eventually closed all its outlets. KFC stayed out of the market for more than ten years, returning on a small scale early in the 1990s.

In product introductions, specialty stores can help generate the keep-up-with-the-neighbors effect. Since most of these stores are specialized by brand instead of by product, they can be effective channels for attracting early adopters.

It doesn't matter if a product is not positioned in a fancy display; Chinese consumers will look for it if they have heard about it. They want complete information, and even specification-like details, next to the product. They read this information carefully to improve their understanding and to gain a feeling of security about the product.

Prime shelf space is also unnecessary. The same product is often found in two locations in a store, with two different prices. There's no better motivation for customers to make a thorough search of the shelves before buying! The makers of Babaozhou, a popular packaged congee mix, never pay a premium for prime shelf space, even when introducing a product. Babaozhou is usually found on the bottom shelves. According to one insider, if the product were promoted with a lot of space in prime spots, consumers might think that something was wrong with it.

Consumers' limited experience with modern marketing makes them depend on reputable brands and track records. The security that brands afford is very impor-

tant in China; in a wide range of goods surveyed, brands
accounted for one-third to one-half of all consumer
expressions of intent to purchase. As one indicator of
brand importance, Chinese consumers usually leave the
makers' tags on the sleeves of their suits and the brand
stickers on their sunglasses.

Trust in brands is enhanced by the media and by
approaches used to promote products. As I mentioned,
the trusted media are those used for official purposes.
Television, radio, and newspapers are tightly controlled
by regulatory bodies, and the public tends to believe
(erroneously) that the regulators have verified all
advertising claims. Moreover, having seen no media
advertising for decades, consumers pay close attention.
Media penetration is high: in Beijing, Shanghai, and
Guangzhou, for example, more than 95% of all households own television sets.

As in the West, a number of household brands are vir-
tual creatures of television buildup. A well-executed
campaign in many major cities is credited for the success
of Apollo, a health drink, whose sales grew at an annual
rate of 290% from 1988 through 1992.

Newspaper advertising can also be very effective.
When an entrepreneur in Guangdong introduced the
Shenzhou ("country of the god") water boiler in 1985, it
attracted little interest. Despite poor sales and weak cash
flow, the entrepreneur managed to borrow 50,000 renminbi from a bank—a large sum for this company—all of
which he spent on ads in newspapers around the country
focusing on the application and benefits of the boiler. In
a few months, the maker had sold out his stock. By 1988,
production had climbed to 200,000 units per year from
1,000 in 1985.

Other marketing approaches, like posters, promotional direct marketing, deep discounts, free trials, and

"free gifts" are ineffective if they are not executed properly. Posters were used in the Cultural Revolution to denounce opponents and more recently by university students to express disagreement with government policies. Therefore, the public associates this marketing technique with unofficial propaganda, which is not to be trusted.

Promotional gimmicks run afoul of a deep cultural bias: they are alien to *guo qing*. A promotion cheapens the product, the Chinese believe, and "cheap products are never good." Suspicion of the idea of getting something for nothing dates back to the fourteenth century, when the Hans launched a rebellion against the Mongolian Yuans by giving away special cakes, inside of which were slips of paper carrying messages to the Hans about the planned uprising.

For all their long-suppressed aspirations to acquire washing machines, cars, and other luxury goods, the Chinese still place a strong emphasis on products that deliver value and satisfy *guo qing*. Because of their cramped living quarters in the cities, for example, consumers go to great lengths to save space. Women like to use two-in-one shampoos and conditioners, and three-in-one cosmetics. Severe urban air pollution forces women to reapply their makeup from time to time; small packages and integrated solutions meet this special need. There are several videocassette recorders on the market whose sales are lagging because they offer too many functions that buyers do not use. Consumers believe that they can't be getting good value when a simpler product would meet their needs.

The varying success of foreign marketers depends on their aggressiveness in brand development and the competitiveness of local manufacturers. It is interesting to note the categories in which foreign marketers have been most successful. (See the chart, "Where Foreign Brands Have Penetrated.")

Given that a marketer needs a deep understanding of Chinese consumers' tastes and habits to succeed in food products, it's no wonder that no foreign multinational has cracked the food business in a big way except Coca-Cola and PepsiCo. No foreign bicycle maker has wrested a competitive advantage from local manufacturers (except for tiny niche segments like high-tech mountain bikes); but in motorcycles, foreign manufacturers maintain a quality advantage over domestic producers.

In the personal care and clothing category, P&G, Unilever, Nike, and Adidas introduced radically new products (compared with the local varieties) that increased the foreign penetration of shampoos, soaps, and athletic shoes to new heights.

On the other hand, Chinese consumers do not find foreign detergent, toothpaste, and cosmetics attractive because domestic producers are upgrading their products quickly and leveraging their market positions to gain superior distribution access. This situation may change if foreign multinationals intensify their market development efforts and better exploit their technology and marketing capabilities.

Targeting Key Cities

As soon as many people in China have become accustomed to owning household appliances and gadgets, their interest is expected to shift to housing (the purchase and furnishing of residences), transportation (cars and motorcycles), and telecommunications (telephones with attachments and electronic gear). This is already

Where Foreign Brands Have Penetrated

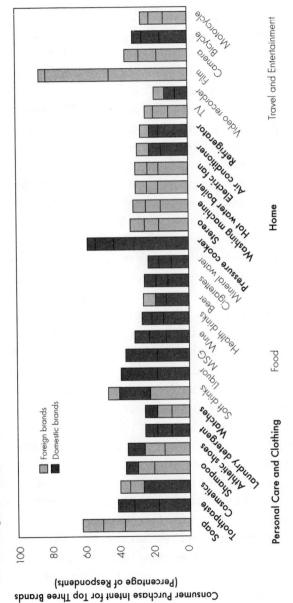

Source: State Statistical Bureau, random sample of people on the street.

happening in a few large cities where income growth is in the double digits.

Most consumer markets in China are very fragmented because of the central-planning philosophy (which emphasizes self-sufficiency at a local level for all products), the inefficient transportation infrastructure, and local government protection of state- and collectively owned businesses. Beijing has announced its intention to consolidate industries and nurture conglomerates, which may mean more vigorous competition for foreigners. To maintain their stakes in consolidating markets, Western companies must target aggressive market-share gains in the coming years. A company trying to double its share in five years should quadruple sales in that period.

Given today's fragmentation, Western marketers must pay close attention to the question of where to enter. An entry strategy concentrated on Guangzhou, Shanghai, and Beijing is almost certain to be inadequate in making a dent and achieving economies of scale; yet a countrywide approach is far too ambitious. A focus on 15 to 20 cities offers the best opportunities. For one food product, 19 key cities, accounting for 15% of the total population and 22% of GNP, had 40% of unit product sales and 90% of the potential profit pool.

The number and location of priority cities depend in the long run on government policy and foreign investment patterns. The central government controls the development of open cities and special economic zones, which in turn drives economic expansion. Investment from neighboring countries also plays a role: Hong Kong in Guangdong, Taiwan in Fujian, and Korea and Japan in the northeast and on the Shandong Peninsula. China is likely to develop a pattern similar to that in the United States, with multiple economic centers along its east coast.

In terms of per capita GNP, the more advanced Chinese coastal cities are still 20 years behind Hong Kong. In view of the current rates of investment by Western businesses and reinvestment in local production for local consumption, the advanced coastal cities may catch up with Hong Kong in a decade or so.

The number of cities a brand manager can target simultaneously depends on local capabilities. How many cities do even old China hands know well, and how many are they willing or able to visit regularly? Most foreign joint ventures focus on three to five key cities along the coast. But bargains in those areas, like Shanghai, are diminishing as land prices and other costs rise. Negotiating for majority control of a joint venture is also very difficult unless the deal includes significant technology transfers.

Concentrating first on three to five key cities, then building sales, distribution, and manufacturing capabilities over a wider area, brand marketers that have gained access can expect rapid growth in conjunction with the following developments: continued economic expansion, which turns more cities into attractive markets; improved distribution networks in secondary cities; the modernization of transportation infrastructure between cities; increased premium segment penetration as consumer wealth in the cities grows and manufacturer-driven marketing campaigns realize expected benefits; and improved cost positions for marketers through investment in local manufacturing.

For multinationals already operating in China, the imperative is to expand beyond the 3-to-5-city entry level. For them the challenge is to cover 15 to 20 key cities by the end of this century.

Obtaining reliable market data, however, is difficult. An enormous system collects and analyzes information for central planning purposes—the State Statistical Bureau alone has 60,000 employees—but information is difficult to extract because it is scattered among various agencies (including commissions, ministries, national corporations, and industry councils), and the "right" person to dispense the data in a particular agency may be unidentifiable. A Westerner who approaches a ministry for help is likely to be referred to the foreign affairs department. Industry-specific market analysis can be undertaken, but the results may be crude. It may take a few hours to examine an industry yearbook or several months to conduct interviews with customers and manufacturers.

As the government monopoly breaks down and more private-enterprise and government-sanctioned businesses take hold, new markets and distribution channels are forming swiftly. The challenge for Western marketers is to understand the driving forces, identify the most likely outcome, and establish a reasonable range of scenarios while recognizing the potential for discontinuity and other risk factors. They may be as familiar to developing nations as inflation and political instability or as idiosyncratic to China as the elements of *guo qing*.

Originally published in September–October 1994
Reprint 94511

Trouble in Paradise

KATHERINE XIN AND VLADIMIR PUCIK

Executive Summary

LIFE IN SHANGHAI HAS BEEN more than comfortable for Mike Graves, the general manager of a U.S. apparel company's 50/50 joint venture with a Chinese manufacturer. His children go to the best school, he lives in a beautiful expat neighborhood, and his company pays for a chauffeur and a nanny. Mike has made the joint venture into a big success, at least in the eyes of its Chinese executives and local officials. Zhong-Lian Knitting has turned around three money-losing businesses and has increased its payroll from 400 to 2,300 employees.

But Mike's boss, the CEO of the U.S. company, Heartland Spindle, doesn't share the rosy view. "A 4% ROI is pathetic," he says. "The numbers should be better by now." He's looking for a 20% ROI, which he says will require laying off 1,200 Chinese workers. He also wants to aim at the high end of the clothing market, meaning

the JV will have to meet much tougher standards of quality than it has been able to do so far.

To make matters worse, the Chinese executives now
want to make a fourth acquisition, which they hope will
position the venture to start its own brand of apparel—a
move that could eat into profits for years.

Can Mike keep the joint venture from unraveling?

Four commentators offer expert advice in this fictional
case study: Eric Jugier, the chairman of Michelin (China)
Investment in Shanghai; Dieter Turowski, a managing
director in Mergers & Acquisitions at Morgan Stanley in
London; David Xu, a principal at McKinsey in Shanghai;
and Paul W. Beamish, the director of the Asian Management Institute at the University of Western Ontario's
Richard Ivey School of Business in Canada.

F ROM MIKE GRAVES'S tall windows, which were
draped in red velvet, the view of Shanghai was spectacu-
lar: the stately old Western-style buildings, the riot of
modern skyscrapers, the familiar needle of the TV tower.
But today Mike barely noticed it. Clenching a copy of his
Chinese partner's proposal for another acquisition—it
would be the company's fourth—he paced the floor and
replayed in his mind that morning's unsettling phone call.

He had called his boss, Bill Windler, at headquarters
in Ohio, hoping to get a nice quote to inject into the brief
remarks he was to make at that day's banquet celebrat-
ing the joint venture's tenth anniversary. But as he gave
Windler a quick rundown of what he intended to say—
mostly about the joint venture's progress toward "world-
class quality"—Mike could sense his boss's growing frus-

tration. About five minutes into the call, Windler cut Mike off in midsentence, saying, "Don't throw your shoulder out patting yourself on the back."

Windler reminded Mike about the margins he was looking for across all of Heartland Spindle's businesses. "A 4% ROI is pathetic," Windler said. "We've been in there ten years, Mike. The numbers should look better by now." He said he was looking for a 20% ROI, adding that such a number could surely be achieved through greater efficiency and more automation. And in Windler's view, the company had at least 1,200 employees too many. "That needs to be fixed, fast," he said.

Mike knew his boss wouldn't take no for an answer, but he had also learned that his Chinese partners would never agree to drastic moves such as the layoffs suggested by Windler. It was beginning to look as though the five good years he had spent here as general manager might be destined to come to a painful end. Mike couldn't help but wonder if those harsh words from Ohio were a warning that his contract might not be renewed in six months.

Then, to top things off, just as Mike had extricated himself from the phone conversation, this latest acquisition proposal had arrived from deputy general manager Qinlin Li. The top executive on the Chinese side of the joint venture, Qinlin had been with the JV since its inception. As before, there would be almost irresistible pressure to go along with the deal. The Chinese side would make it clear yet again that the delicate partnership depended on Mike's support for continuous expansion and protection of jobs. The timing couldn't have been worse: The last thing Windler would want was more growth initiatives eating into the profits.

A knock on the heavy teak door snapped him out of his musings. Feng Chen, Mike's assistant and translator, informed him that his car was waiting.

Enhance Friendly Cooperation

As the car pulled up outside the Shangri-La Hotel, Mike forced himself to smile at the red carpet lined with dozens of lavish flower baskets sent by local government officials, business partners, suppliers, customers, and even competitors. A marching band in full uniform stood at the hotel entrance, and above it stretched a bright red banner that said, in Chinese and English: "Enhance Friendly Cooperation and Ensure Mutual Growth" and "Celebrate the Tenth Anniversary of Zhong-Lian Knitting Co. Ltd."

Mike exchanged greetings with Qinlin, who had been there for an hour already and was still seeing to last-minute details. In the ballroom, an elegant young woman in a red silk *qi-pao*, a traditional dress for formal celebrations, escorted Mike to the round table that was front and center. Two Chinese senior executives, Qinlin's immediate subordinates, stood up and nodded their greetings.

There was a burst of excited applause, and cameras flashed. Qinlin was accompanying three important government officials into the room. They approached Mike's table and politely bickered for several minutes over who should enjoy the most prominent seat at the table, as required by Chinese custom. At last, the eldest and most highly placed official accepted the seat of honor. Qinlin stepped up to the podium, above which hung a huge Chinese knot of red silk, the symbol of cooperation. There was an expectant hush as he tapped the microphone.

"Ladies and gentlemen," Qinlin began, "thank you for joining me to celebrate the tenth anniversary of Zhong-Lian Knitting Company Limited. Those who were with the company at the beginning remember the hardships we endured and the hard work we put in. Since the establishment of Zhong-Lian as a 50/50 joint venture between Suzhou First Textile Company and our U.S. partner, Heartland Spindle Company, Zhong-Lian has faced many difficulties and obstacles. But we succeeded." Mike was listening to the translator's words, but he could hear the passion in Qinlin's voice. "We turned a money-losing company into a money-making company, and we made great headway as a result of support from our government, efforts on the part of both parent companies, and all our managers and employees."

Mike hadn't been there during the early days, but he knew the stories. He was the fourth GM sent by Heartland in ten years. His two most recent predecessors had left before their three-year assignments were complete, one for family reasons—his wife couldn't adapt to China—and the other for a better job offer (allegedly). Mike, a veteran manager with 20 years of international experience, had lived and worked in Japan, Hong Kong, and Australia before Heartland sent him to Shanghai.

Mike's toughest challenge at the outset was the language barrier. He wouldn't have survived without Feng Chen's help. It didn't take long for Mike to learn what *cha-bu-duo* meant: "almost okay." He hated that word! It was baffling to him: Even though his Chinese partners were intelligent and willing to work hard, they weren't exactly obsessed with quality. They cut corners and hardly ever followed operating procedures to the letter. Buttons often fell off sweaters before the garments were even shipped out of the factory. *Cha-bu-duo* is why Mike insisted on introducing Total Quality Management to Zhong-Lian—and TQM was probably why the JV had been so successful. Mike had also felt a small sense of satisfaction when he taught his Chinese colleagues a new term: Six Sigma.

Cha-bu-duo wasn't the only expression Mike heard all too often. He also quickly got used to *yan-jiu-yan-jiu*, which means "Let's review and discuss." When he proposed a new system to deal with sewage disposal three months after he started (he was astonished that his Chinese partner hadn't updated it already), his counterparts said, "Okay, *yan-jiu-yan-jiu*." Two months later, after Mike's repeated prodding, the proposal made it onto a meeting agenda. But at the meeting, the Chinese managers seemed reluctant to discuss the matter, and no one wanted to assume responsibility for solving the problem. When Mike asked managers for feedback individually, they all had ideas, many of them excellent. He couldn't imagine why the managers hadn't spoken up at the meeting.

It didn't make sense to him until months later, when Mike heard someone say, "Keeping silent in a group is safer. You won't get in trouble if you don't do anything. But you will get in trouble if you make a mistake. We are experienced under this system, and we know how it works." At any rate, Mike was relieved when the equipment was set up—even though it took two years and outside pressure from the provincial Environment Protection Bureau to make it happen.

There was another burst of applause. Qinlin's voice reverberated through the room. "We have acquired three money-losing state-owned enterprises and managed to earn an annual profit of between 5% and 6%," he said. "The number of employees increased from 400 to 2,300

in the past decade. Given the slump of the textile industry in these years, Zhong-Lian's achievement is remarkable. In the coming years, we will further enhance the
company and maintain our growth momentum."

Qinlin paused, and his eyes sparkled. "Let me tell you
another piece of good news," he said. "We are preparing
our fourth acquisition, which is expected to raise our
production capacity by 40%. The number of our employees will grow to nearly 3,500. And all this will help us
launch our next initiative: building our own *national
brand*."

What little appetite Mike had for the celebration van-
ished. He had long been trying to quash that kind of talk.
Heartland, he knew, would never support launching an
apparel brand that would eat up resources and limit
profits for years. Qinlin knows this well, Mike thought, so
why is he raising expectations in such a public way?

Qinlin thanked the vice mayor and the other government officials without whose "wise supervision," in his
effusive words, the joint venture would not have made
such great progress. The vice mayor rose to speak and
returned the compliments, praising Zhong-Lian's contribution to the local economy—especially to maintaining
employment levels—and calling the joint venture a flag-
ship among the city's enterprises.

When it was Mike's turn, he too voiced the expected
praise for the officials—it was a ritual whose airy forms
and steely seriousness had become almost second nature
to him. But throughout his little speech, he felt he was
hardly doing more than going through the motions. He
was preoccupied by Qinlin's plans and what they would
mean for profitability.

Later, the lazy Susan at each table was filled with
eight cold dishes, eight hot dishes, and two showpiece

dishes: a whole suckling pig and a whole braised mandarin fish in the shape of a squirrel. Qinlin, as the host of his table, proposed a toast. Then he emptied his glass as a sign of his sincerity and joy. Glasses clinked; champagne and Coke bubbled. But Mike had become so attuned to the subtleties of these gatherings that he immediately noticed the response of the officials: Instead of emptying their glasses, they merely took sips. Mike supposed that they must have heard about his opposition, muted though it had been, to the expansion ideas.

Living in Style

Sitting in the backseat of the company car, Mike felt his tension ease when his driver, Lao Li, turned into his neighborhood. The car slipped by a row of cypresses and passed a perfectly manicured golf course. Designed in European country style, the elegant Green Villa was an ideal residence for expatriates. Mike loved this village— its extensive recreational amenities, its first-class service. At very little cost, for example, Mike's family had hired a live-in domestic helper who happened to be a superior cook. His wife, Linda, played golf three times a week with her friends in the village, and she had recently taken up yoga. The company paid $7,800 a month to rent the family's home; it also paid for a chauffeur, a nanny, and the children's education at Concordia International School (the best in Shanghai). Life here was easy and comfortable—a world away from what it would have been like back in Ohio.

But Mike's tension returned when he thought about his meeting the next morning with the people at Hua-Ying, the potential acquisition. He wouldn't be living in Green Villa much longer if he signed off on that deal.

Over dinner, Mike told Linda about the conversation with Windler.

"Don't they understand that the Chinese way of doing business is different from the American way?" Linda asked him sympathetically. "It's not all about squeezing the most out of your workers here. They value stability and long-term employment. You'd think Heartland would've been prepared for this sort of performance. It's not like you're losing money, like so many JVs here do. Just last week on the course, Christie and Maya told me that their husbands' businesses hadn't turned a profit yet."

"I know, but that doesn't seem to be good enough any more," Mike said. He recounted Bill's suggestions about layoffs and investing in more automated equipment. He knew that he would soon have to broach these subjects with his Chinese partners.

Mike's biggest problem was that he could see both sides. Heartland wanted to reposition itself in the U.S. market—selling at discount stores wasn't profitable enough. But to enable Heartland to make the jump to high-end retailers, the joint venture would have to meet much higher standards of quality. Those old dyeing machines, for instance, would have to go; they had cost the company a lot of money over the last few years, not just in shipping and handling charges for returned products but also in terms of the company's reputation. New machines would fix that problem, but they'd create another one: Many jobs would disappear.

The Chinese partners were much more concerned with creating jobs and keeping government officials happy than with improving quality. They wanted to keep growing into new provinces and buying up unprofitable companies, even if turning them around took years. But expansion would require significant additional resources that Heartland Spindle clearly wasn't ready to commit. And now there would be pressure to create a new company to market a national brand, again a drain on cash.

"So what do you think you're going to do?" Linda asked.

"I'm meeting with executives from Hua-Ying tomorrow morning. Maybe they'll surprise me with an operation that won't take forever to turn around—that'd be the best case," Mike said. "After that, I'll have to talk to Qinlin and the others about Heartland's concerns. But I know how that conversation will play out. They'll say Heartland is being shortsighted and that the JV's history of turning around money-losing businesses should prove that we just need to be more patient.

"I wish Bill and the rest back in the States had a better understanding of how things work here. I was skeptical myself at the beginning. Remember when we first got here and I was fuming at the business expenses? Seemed like every executive on the payroll was wining and dining some key partner or contact. And Robert O'Reilly, our controller, came to me shouting that our Chinese partner spent money like water. But, gradually, we both figured out that those expenses were paying off for us. The Chinese ritual of sharing food—nurturing *guanxi*—is so powerful in making deals that it became one of our hidden assets. I'm afraid we won't get those kinds of results if we focus only on cutting costs and laying off workers, as Ohio wants us to do."

PowerPoint and Green Tea

The chief executive of Hua-Ying, Genfa Wang, sent his own limousine to pick up Mike and Qinlin as a symbol of his sincerity and hospitality. Genfa and his top managers were waiting at the gate when the car pulled up, and one of the men stepped forward to open the car door. Genfa greeted Mike, Qinlin, and Feng Chen with, "My honor! My honor! It is a great pleasure to have you here with us."

The first building they entered looked fairly clean, but the conference room carpet was pocked with cigarette burns. Not exactly a high-class operation, Mike thought. Up on the third floor, there was a disagreeable odor—no flush. He could just imagine the state of the plumbing. And hadn't leaky pipes been responsible for the initial spread of SARS into cities in Hong Kong? He was sure he had read something like that. His unease grew. What other hidden risks were lurking in this facility? There was no way he was going to be able to agree to this acquisition, he thought.

But he was pleasantly surprised to see seven cups of Bi Luo Chun tea, one of the best Chinese green teas, on an elegant redwood table. And a minute later, Genfa pulled out a laptop and began making his presentation using PowerPoint slides. Mike was shocked. He hadn't expected such sophistication from a company this size, especially a company that seemed to lack modern sanitary facilities. Genfa, sensing Mike's reaction, said proudly, "My nephew gave me training on this high-tech stuff. He is a college graduate, a vice GM of our company in charge of technology and engineering."

Great, Mike thought with exasperation. There were probably a few relatives on the board, too. But his mood swung back during Genfa's 40-minute presentation as the CEO spoke precisely and clearly about the numbers—it was obvious he was shrewd about the market. Mike was intrigued.

At the second building, his earlier impressions were reinforced: The machines in here looked old and shabby. Some workers were busy, but others were idly waiting for a product delivery. Bales of goods were stacked high in one corner, and Mike stumbled over a box as he picked his way through the dim light. When he noticed that the record sheets on the desk and walls were handwritten, his heart sank: So much for high tech.

On his way home that night in his own company's car, Mike gazed out the window, trying to figure out what to do next. Should he recommend the acquisition to Bill? Should he propose rejecting the deal and thus probably bring an end to the partnership? The idea of buying out the JV had occurred to him, but it clearly wouldn't work, not with the Chinese partner dreaming of a national brand. When the Audi came to a stop outside Mike's house, he hadn't reached any conclusions. He knew he was going to have another sleepless night at Green Villa.

Can Mike keep the joint venture from unraveling?

Four commentators offer expert advice.

ERIC JUGIER *is the chairman of Michelin (China) Investment in Shanghai.*

Mike Graves needs to do four things, and quickly. First, he needs to develop a clearer vision of Heartland Spindle's—and its partners'—strategic goals in China. Second, he needs to assemble a much stronger team for the company. Third, he needs to consider alternatives to the traditional 50/50 joint venture. And, finally, he needs to move outside his personal comfort zone as a manager.

The lack of a clear, shared strategy is the most glaring problem in this case. Is Heartland chiefly interested in China as a low-cost production base for U.S. exports? Or is it hoping to win a share of the domestic market? If so, which segment is Heartland focusing on—and based on what competitive edge?

Without a clear strategy, it's impossible to choose the right structure for and extent of cooperation with a foreign partner. Conversely, when your intent is clear and reasonable, you can get past a surprising number of obstacles. When Michelin started discussions in Shanghai with China's largest tire manufacturer, we were clear that we intended to develop a major center there for the world tire industry and that we would therefore have to bring our best technology. To protect that technology, we would need control of the venture, which initially seemed impossible to achieve from a legal standpoint. As it turned out, we got control because the municipality shared the goal and recognized the necessity.

Perhaps there once was a clear strategy that has been forgotten over the course of ten years and several changes in management. Mike should study the contracts and, more important, have discussions with the original sponsors of the deal. If he can learn the initial intentions, he might find a positive starting point for rebuilding a spirit of cooperation with his partner.

This brings me to my second point: the importance of mobilizing a team of people to further the JV's strategy. Political officials are going to be a big part of that team; they have a stronger influence on economic life in China than Mike might realize. He must reach out to them and understand their goals. It is not a matter of good dinners and dubious expenses left to the Chinese staff. Success will depend on the personal involvement of top executives. I cannot overstress how crucial relationships are in China. Only when individuals know and understand each other can they develop the level of cooperation required for success.

Mike should convince his boss to be the one who owns the relationship with a key official—the vice mayor, say. Yes, this will add a layer of complexity, but success in China is as much about time as it is about money. This is the most important fact for Mike to impress upon the leadership back at headquarters. Our CEO, Edouard Michelin, is in the habit of coming to China two or three times a year, with a flexible agenda, and that does a great deal to develop and support our operations here.

Mike also needs to think creatively about alternatives to the traditional 50/50 joint venture. For instance, if Heartland Spindle is focused on exports and profitability, it might make more sense to have a minority share in the venture. Heartland would bring know-how to the table and would purchase the export production, leaving the Chinese partner to manage productivity and profit levels. That would protect Heartland's margins and reduce its investment, yielding a higher return on assets.

The point is that this situation might require a creative solution, and that brings me to my final concern. Mike needs to move out of his comfort zone and learn to strategize and negotiate in a highly dynamic environment. He should be the one taking the initiative, not reacting in surprise to the ideas and actions of others.

DIETER TUROWSKI *is a managing director in Mergers & Acquisitions at Morgan Stanley in London.*

It's never easy making joint ventures work, especially when the strategic objectives of the partners diverge. Zhong-Lian Knitting has had a very successful ten years, during which the partners have been able to work out their differences. But this JV may well have outlived its usefulness.

Zhong-Lian is similar to many other joint ventures in that its problems are partly due to its success. I am reminded of the JV created in the early 1980s by Merck and the Swedish pharmaceutical company Astra to help Astra enter the U.S. market. It operated successfully for more than a decade; by the late 1990s, various analysts estimated it to be worth up to $10 billion, largely because of sales of the blockbuster drug Prilosec. But the parties increasingly found that their objectives were incompatible. Merck wanted to continue benefiting from Astra's current products and R&D pipeline, but Astra needed control over its U.S. operations to pursue its vision of becoming a leading global pharmaceutical company. The partners eventually agreed to restructure the venture so that Astra had control, and Merck would receive payments based on the sales of future products. Zhong-Lian and its Chinese parent, Suzhou First Textile, may be at a similar crossroads.

To determine his next step, Mike Graves needs to answer a fundamental question: Have the partners' strategic interests moved so far apart that the JV no longer makes sense in its current form? The answer appears to be yes. Suzhou is focused on expansion within China and on developing a national brand; this strategy will continue to put pressure on the venture's financial performance. Heartland Spindle is focused on short- to medium-term financial returns and on transforming Zhong-Lian into a high-quality manufacturer. No amount of discussion is going to reconcile their differences.

If he concludes that the status quo is not viable, Mike must ask himself a second question: How can he restructure or exit the JV in a way that makes sense for Heartland? To answer, he must take into account any termination or exit clauses in the joint venture agreement. He must also determine whether Heartland needs to have an ownership interest in the JV to continue the commercial relationship with it and whether Suzhou is financially able to buy out Heartland's interest in the JV.

Mike would be well advised to investigate several options in parallel. They could include selling some or all of Heartland's interest to Suzhou. A phased exit in which Heartland reduces its ownership stake over time could make sense if Heartland wants to minimize disruption in the relationship; it might also make it easier for Suzhou to raise capital (if this is a constraint). Alternatively, Mike could explore the sale of Heartland's interest to a more compatible third party. The partners might also wish to consider an IPO, assuming that Zhong-Lian is sufficiently developed to make this option realistic. An IPO would give Heartland an exit while providing the joint venture access to capital to continue its growth.

A third question Mike should be asking is, What is Heartland's overall joint venture strategy, not just in China but also in other markets? Heartland should consider establishing a portfolio of joint venture relationships in China and other low-cost regions. That would allow the company to diversify its sourcing relationships, reducing the risk associated with any one partner. It would also allow Heartland to upgrade its skills in establishing and managing international joint ventures. Perhaps if Mike's boss became involved in negotiating a few international JVs, he would acquire a better appreciation for the challenges involved in managing such relationships.

DAVID XU *is a principal at management consulting firm McKinsey & Company in Shanghai.*

Heartland Spindle entered the China market at the same time many multinationals did, about a decade ago, seeing the same enormous opportunity. The market was huge and there was undercapacity in many segments and industries, so high margins seemed assured. But that was a shortsighted and static view of the market. As the multinationals rushed in and productivity quickly improved, the immediate result was a dramatic expansion of capacity, and margins deteriorated. In very short order, the companies' expectations about revenues and profits became obsolete.

Heartland also went the usual route of entering China by means of a joint venture. Many multinationals chose this path because of regulation requirements, others because of their unfamiliarity with the Chinese business landscape. Many of them have come to regret that decision. In a McKinsey survey of executives of foreign companies in China three years ago, a great number of respondents said that if they were to move into China again, they would do so through a solely owned business, not a joint venture. The main reason was that the partners often don't share the same vision or philosophy, and the disparity in the viewpoints hampers performance. The survey also found that more than half of the joint ventures in China are not working properly.

In Zhong-Lian's case, the problem does not seem to be the cultural difference so much as the difference in the two partners' visions and definitions of success. One question, then, is whether Heartland's high-margin vision is sensible. The textile industry in China is extremely competitive and will be for the foreseeable future because the entry barriers are low. The margins in textiles are therefore typically very low, except for special textiles and products with very strong brands. My first advice to Mike Graves would be to study the industry structure closely and determine whether a 20% return on investment is theoretically possible for Zhong-Lian's products.

The next question is whether this joint venture is in a position to capture the highest margin in its industry. Does it have a unique business model, perhaps, based on some core competence? Maybe it can leverage its channel or its brand back in the United States or in other developed markets. Or perhaps Heartland can make the venture a bigger part of its global strategy, exploiting the region's labor costs and productivity edge to reconfigure its worldwide production strategy.

If Mike doesn't discover a unique business model that will generate a 20% ROI, he needs to inform his boss that it's time to exit. But if he believes such a return is achievable, he needs to restructure the JV to get there. If Heartland doesn't want to make any more of an investment in the venture, it could bring in a private shareholder or other market-driven companies to buy the government's shares. Mike also needs to ensure that he is linking compensation packages to performance. I've observed that employees in China—especially senior managers—respond very, very well to pay-for-performance plans.

It's been my experience that Chinese organizations are quite adaptable to other cultures. The problem here, and perhaps for many companies, is that real assimilation can't occur unless the two partners are working toward the same goals. Zhong-Lian is under the strong influence of the government, and, as a result, it is doing exactly what should be expected: creating jobs and boosting revenue rather than profits. The minute Mike starts to create a market-driven and value-creation-driven company—largely by rewarding senior managers for gains in those directions—things will start to change.

The joint venture is already one of the success stories on the Chinese business landscape. If the venture is restructured and incentives are aligned with higher performance, it might even meet the expectations Heartland has set for it.

PAUL W. BEAMISH *is the director of the Asian Management Institute at the Richard Ivey School of Business of the University of Western Ontario in London, Ontario.*

Mike Graves needs to start by acknowledging that his boss is correct: A 4% ROI is not enough for most foreign investors after ten years. So where is the problem? Is it in the Chinese market itself? Is it with the partnership agreement? Or is it with Mike? I'd argue that all three contribute to this dilemma.

Let's look at the Chinese market first. Many foreign companies are finding it tough to generate acceptable profits there. Even the Japanese, historically the biggest investors, are seeing their lowest returns in China. (And when the Japanese do invest, the size of their subsidiaries tends to be smaller; they don't employ anywhere near the number of people Zhong-Lian Knitting does.)

China is also becoming a more expensive place to do business. Between 1992 and 2001, the consumer price index in the United States increased by 1.27 times; in Shanghai, it went up 2.21 times. Wage rates in Shanghai more than tripled between 1991 and 2000. It's not surprising that more and more competitive Japanese corporations have begun to pull out of the market—they are a little further along the "exit curve" than Bill Windler is.

Next, the partnership. In any international joint venture, the partners must share congruent performance measures. That is certainly not the case here. While both partners have an explicit goal that the JV be profitable, they differ widely in terms of what constitutes an acceptable financial return. Furthermore, some of their nonfinancial goals for the JV seem to have evolved and have only now become explicit. The Chinese partner is happy with achieving a 5% to 6% profit and being viewed as a local hero. It wants to grow the scope of the JV and establish a national brand. The U.S. partner wants a 20% ROI, will consider growth only if it improves profitability, has no interest in creating employment unless it improves the bottom line, wants to improve quality, and sees no benefit to creating a Chinese brand because it views China as a low-cost manufacturing platform rather than a market. In the absence of congruent performance objectives, the joint venture has no underlying strategic logic. Thus the partners immediately need to revisit both their older and continuing reasons for staying together. If the partners cannot agree on a minimally acceptable ROI or that such a goal is a top priority, they should think about exiting the venture.

Finally, Mike is part of the problem. It is absolutely stunning that he learned on the day of the anniversary banquet that his partner wanted to make another acquisition. Either the Chinese partner is out of control or Mike is out of touch. How much time is Mike spending with the partner? Has he grown too comfortable in paradise?

Mike needs to be proactive. Rather than simply waiting for his Chinese partner to hand him the names of acquisition candidates, for instance, he could develop specific acquisition criteria with his partner or even conduct some investigations himself. He should also look for additional ways of improving the JV's profitability. One of the largest costs in many joint ventures in China is the expatriate manager package. He could save money by reducing the number of expats, perhaps by promoting local managers. Lots of smart people are available.

Various factors have contributed to the current situation, some of which—such as the condition of the Chinese market—Mike cannot control. He needs to concentrate on the things he can change: the relationship between the U.S. and Chinese partners and his own managerial behavior.

Originally published in August 2003
Reprint R0308A

The Forgotten Strategy

PANKAJ GHEMAWAT

Executive Summary

MOST MULTINATIONALS SEE globalization as a matter of replication—spreading a single business model as widely as possible to maximize economies of scale. From this perspective, the key strategic challenge is choosing how much of the model to keep standard and how much to grudgingly adapt to local tastes. But focusing exclusively on that choice is a mistake, for it blinds companies to the very real opportunities they can still gain from arbitrage—from exploiting differences as opposed to similarities.

Indeed, the scope for arbitrage is as wide as the differences that remain among countries, and those differences continue to be broad and deep. They can, in fact, be divided into four main categories—cultural, administrative, economic, and geographic. In each category, old opportunities persist and new ones are arising, sometimes very quickly. Consider the continued cachet of French culture in its wines and haute couture. Witness, too, how swiftly the Finns have become known for their expertise in wireless communications. Clearly, legal and other administrative differences, particularly in tax laws and the cost of capital, remain large. So do purely economic wage differentials, especially for knowledge workers and other skilled employees. And if modern transportation and other technologies have reduced geographic advantages and brought down the price of spices, they've also made possible expanded trade in other goods like perishable flowers and out-of-season produce.

Both the differences that make arbitrage valuable and the similarities that make replication important will remain with us for the foreseeable future, and combining the two, while necessary, is tricky. But that spells competitive advantage for those companies that have the imagination to see the full range of possibilities.

TEN YEARS AGO, globalization seemed unstoppable. Today, the picture looks very different. Even Coca-Cola, widely seen as a standard-bearer of global business, has had its doubts about an idea it once took for granted. It was a Coke CEO, the late Roberto Goizueta, who declared in 1996: "The labels 'international' and 'domestic' . . . no longer apply." His globalization program, often summarized under the tagline "think global, act global," had included an unprecedented amount of standardization. By the time he passed away in 1997, Coca-Cola derived 67% of its revenues and 77% of its profits from outside North America.

But Goizueta's strategy soon ran into trouble, due in large part to the Asian currency crisis. By the end of 1999, when Douglas Daft took the reins, earnings had slumped, and Coke's stock had lost nearly one-third of its peak market value—a loss of about $70 billion. Daft's solution was an aggressive shift in the opposite direction. On taking over, he avowed, "The world in which we operate has changed dramatically, and we must change to succeed. . . . No one drinks globally. Local people get thirsty and . . . buy a locally made Coke."

Unfortunately, "local" didn't seem to be any better a description of Coke's market space than "global." On March 7, 2002, the *Asian Wall Street Journal* announced: "After two years of lackluster sales . . . the "think local, act local" mantra is gone. Oversight over marketing is returning to Atlanta."

If the business climate can force Coke, which historically was (and is) more profitable internationally than domestically, to seesaw back and forth on globalization in this way, think of the pressures on the typical large company, for which international business is usually much less profitable than domestic business, as the sidebar "A Poor Global Showing" reveals.

Why is globalization proving so hard to get right? The answer is related in part to how companies frame their globalization strategies. In many if not most cases, companies see globalization as a matter of taking a superior (by assumption) business model and extending it geographically, with necessary modifications, to maximize the firm's economies of scale. From this perspective, the key strategic challenge is simply to determine how much to adapt the business model—how much to standardize from country to country versus how much to localize to respond to local differences. Recently, as at Coke, many companies have moved toward more localization and less standardization. But no matter how they balance localization and standardization, all companies that view

---

A Poor Global Showing

Since 1990, the foreign operations of large companies have consistently posted lower average returns on sales than their domestic operations. Nor do foreign revenues work as a hedge against slumping domestic results. As the graph below clearly shows, foreign and domestic margins generally move in the same direction. Based on data supplied by Michael Gestrin of the OECD, the graph compares the foreign and domestic operating margins for 147 of the companies in the Fortune Global 500 for which such data were available for at least six years.

Of course, an international presence could theoretically add value even if international operations were persistently less profitable, in accounting terms, than domestic operations. Say, for instance, that significant fixed costs incurred at home can be avoided by entering foreign markets. But other recent studies, based on market values rather than accounting data, also tend to indicate that, on average, an international presence impairs performance instead of improving it.

Such studies are certainly subject to many caveats (about data, inferences of causality, and so on). And in any case, they reflect average tendencies around which there is substantial—and predictable—variation. So one should not conclude from them that individual companies ought never expand beyond their home countries. A more sensible lesson to draw is that companies need to think harder about how globalization can add value instead of assuming that if they are profitable at home, they will surely be profitable abroad.

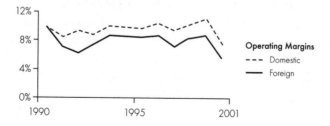

global strategy in this way focus on similarities across countries, and the potential for the scale economies that such commonalities unlock, as their primary source of added value. Differences from country to country, in contrast, are viewed as obstacles that need to be overcome.

Correctly choosing how much to adapt a business model is certainly important for extracting value from international operations. But to focus exclusively on the tension between global scale economies and local considerations is a mistake, for it blinds companies to the very real opportunities they could gain from exploiting differences. Indeed, in their rush to exploit the similarities across borders, multinationals have discounted the original global strategy: arbitrage, the strategy of difference.

Of course, we're all familiar with arbitrage in its traditional, and least-sustainable, form—the pure exploitation of price differentials. But the world is not so homogeneous as to have removed arbitrage from a company's strategic tool kit. In fact, many forms of arbitrage offer relatively sustainable sources of competitive advantage, and as some opportunities for arbitrage disappear, others spring up to take their place. I do not claim that arbitrage to exploit differences is any more a complete strategic solution than the optimal exploitation of scale economies. To the contrary: If they are to get their global strategies right in the long term, many companies will have to find ways to combine the two approaches, despite the very real tensions between them. (See "Complex Aggregation Strategies" at the end of this article.)

The Strategy of Differences

Arbitrage gets little respect these days as a global strategy. This partly reflects the tendency of companies to equate size with a global presence, which naturally focuses the mind on scale economies rather than on the absolute economies that underlie arbitrage. But it also reflects the fact that arbitrage has been around for so long. Many of the industries in which arbitrage has historically been applied—farming, mining, and textiles—are regarded as low-tech and mature. There is also the sense that well-run global enterprises have already reaped what competitive advantage they can from arbitraging such generic factors of production as capital or labor, which, as one leading management guru has put it, can now be sourced efficiently with the click of a mouse.

But arbitrage is about much more than cheap capital or labor (although these, as we will see, continue to be very important). Indeed, the scope for arbitrage is as wide as the differences that remain among countries, which continue to be broad and deep. Some of the empirical evidence for this can be found in my last HBR article, "Distance Still Matters: The Hard Reality of Global Expansion" (September 2001), where I presented a four-dimensional framework for measuring distance between countries. I argued that distance could be measured not only by geography but also by the extent of differences in culture, differences in the administrative and institutional context, and differences in economic attributes (which all together I call the CAGE framework).[1] Let us consider each type of arbitrage in turn to examine both the traditional and less obvious ways companies can apply arbitrage strategies to exploit differences.

CULTURAL ARBITRAGE

Arbitrage strategies have in fact long exploited differences in culture. For example, French culture (or, more specifically, its cachet abroad) has long underpinned the international success of French haute couture, cuisine, wines, and perfumes. But cultural arbitrage can also be applied to newer products and services. Consider, for example, the extraordinary international dominance of U.S.-based fast-food chains, which at the end of the 1990s accounted for 27 of the world's top 30 fast-food chains and for over 60% of worldwide fast-food sales. In their international operations, these chains exploit to varying extents the general global surge of American popular culture by serving up slices of Americana (at least as it's perceived locally) along with their food. Nor, certainly, is this advantage reserved for rich nations; many poor countries are important platforms for cultural arbitrage. Think of Haitian compas music and dance music from the Congo, which enjoy image advantages in their respective regions.

Claims that the scope for cultural arbitrage is decreasing over time are clearly not true for all countries and product categories. The persistent association of Brazil with football, carnival, beaches, and sex—which all resonate powerfully in the marketing of youth-oriented products and services—illustrates the unexploited potential of some countries in this regard, though in this case the potential is starting to be recognized. Witness Molson's recent launch in the Canadian market of A Marca Bavaria, a superpremium beer imported from its Brazilian subsidiary, which uses its association with Brazil's high-energy and sensual image to target primarily 19- to 24-year-old men. In fact, new opportunities for reinforcing cultural arbitrage are appearing all the time. For instance, the push by the European Union to restrict labels such as Parma ham and Cognac brandy to only those products that actually come from those places is a move to reinforce the natural advantages of particular geographic areas. What's more, as Finland's recently developed reputation for excellence in wireless technology shows, in certain product categories, such advantages can now be created much faster than before, in years rather than decades or centuries. Reduction in other dimensions of difference—tariffs or transport costs, for instance—can also increase the viability of cultural arbitrage.

ADMINISTRATIVE ARBITRAGE

Legal, institutional, and political differences from country to country open up a host of strategic arbitrage opportunities. Tax differentials are an obvious example. Through the 1990s, to take one case, Rupert Murdoch's News Corporation paid income taxes at an average rate of less than 10%, rather than the statutory 30% to 36% of the three main countries in which it operated: Britain, the United States, and Australia. By comparison, major competitors such as Disney were paying close to the official rates. These tax savings were critical to News Corporation's expansion into the United States, given the profit pressures on the company: net margins consistently less than 10% of sales in the second half of the 1990s and an asset-to-sales ratio that had ballooned to three to one. By placing its U.S. acquisitions into holding companies in the Cayman Islands, News Corporation could deduct interest payments on the debt used to finance the deals against the profits generated from its newspaper operations in Britain. Overall, the company has incorporated approximately 100 subsidiaries in havens with no or low corporate taxes and limited financial disclosure laws. The intangibility of its informational assets has helped in this regard. As one accounting authority puts it: "There's absolutely no reason why a piece of paper, which is the right to show something, couldn't sit anywhere. So it could be sitting in the Cayman Islands."

Few managers ever explicitly treat tax or other administrative arbitrages as a strategic tool, despite their potential. That's partly because executives are reluctant to draw attention to such arrangements for fear that they might be outlawed. For instance, many Chinese businesspeople channel investment funds through foreign third parties and then back into China to secure better legal protection, tax concessions, or otherwise favorable treatment. In fact, about half the foreign direct investment flowing into China is estimated to have originated in China. Similar considerations explain why Mauritius is one of the top two sources of FDI flowing into India.

In some cases, administrative arbitrageurs are actually breaking the law. By some estimates, more than half the regular filter cigarettes smoked in India are smuggled in. Given the taxes and tariffs evaded, they can be sold for 30% to 50% less than cigarettes legally produced and sold there. Major international tobacco companies have been widely accused in the press of conniving in such activities to boost profits and market penetration. And if India has high tariffs, "there is," as the CEO of a candy manufacturer pointed out, "always Dubai" (a major entrepôt and smuggling hub). Clearly, legislation and law enforcement face a huge challenge.

Most forms of administrative arbitrage involve working with or around given rules. In some cases, though, companies can leverage political power to try to change the rules. In 1994, for example, four big Swedish corporations—ABB, Volvo, Ericsson, and Stora—threatened to send overseas as much as $6.6 billion in investments to pressure the Swedish government into limiting corporate tax rates. Similarly, companies can use powerful home governments to pressure foreign governments into granting favorable treatment. Enron, for example, enlisted the help of the Clinton State Department, which obligingly threatened to cut off development assistance to Mozambique, one of the poorest countries in the world, if it granted a gas deal to a South African competitor instead of to an Enron-led consortium. Unattractive though they are, stories like this suggest that the potential for using government influence to create administrative arbitrage opportunities remains high.

GEOGRAPHIC ARBITRAGE

Considering all that has been written about the alleged death of distance, it is hardly surprising that few strategy gurus take geographic arbitrage very seriously. It is true that transportation and communication costs have dropped sharply in the last few decades. But the drop does not necessarily translate into a decrease in the scope of geographic arbitrage strategies. Consider the case of air transportation, the cost of which has declined more than 90% in real terms since 1930, more sharply than older modes of transportation. In the process, new opportunities for geographic arbitrage have been created. For example, in the Netherlands' Aalsmeer international flower market, more than 20 million flowers and 2 million plants are auctioned off every day; blooms flown in from India are sold to customers in the United States or Europe on the day they arrive.

Although communication costs have dropped more sharply than transportation costs, there are cases in the telecom sector where returns earned by focusing on residual distance have been higher than those gained by building or exploiting global connectivity. Cable & Wireless, a far-flung and once high-flying telecom company headquartered in London, has two main areas of business, organized into a regional unit and a global one. Analysts assess the market value of the global unit, in which $10 billion has been invested since 1999, at about zero because competitors also invested in much the same kind of long-haul overcapacity and global connectivity. The valuable part of the company is its regional unit, which consists of subsidiaries providing a full range of telecommunication services to consumer and business customers in 33 small countries around the world— mainly islands, whose communication links with the outside world C&W still dominates.

The geographic arbitrageurs that *have* lost some ground in recent decades are the great general trading companies of the past, which traditionally took advantage of large international variations in prices for a broad array of products by getting them from market A to market B (and in the process somewhat eroding those price differentials). Lower transportation costs and greater connectivity have made it much easier for manufacturers and retailers to exploit these opportunities themselves. Yet the savviest trading companies have found ways to stay in business. For instance, instead of simply engaging in trading, Hong Kong–based Li & Fung derives most of its revenue from a more sophisticated kind of geographic arbitrage, setting up and managing multinational supply chains for clients through its offices in more than 30 countries.

ECONOMIC ARBITRAGE

In a sense, all arbitrage strategies that add value are economic. But I use the term here to refer to exploitation of specific economic factors that don't derive directly from a country's culture, geography, or administrative context. These factors include differences in the costs of labor and capital, as well as variations in more industry-specific inputs such as knowledge or the availability of complementary products, technologies, or infrastructures.

The best-known type of economic arbitrage is the exploitation of cheap labor, which is common in labor-intensive, capital-light industries like clothing. But high-tech, capital-intensive companies can use the strategy just as well. Consider the case of Embraer, the Brazilian firm that, among other types of aircraft, designs and assembles regional jets. Many factors contribute to Embraer's success, including managerial and technical excellence, but labor arbitrage has clearly played a critical role. Witness Embraer's employment costs, which came to $26,000 per employee in 2002, versus an estimated $63,000 in the regional jet business of its chief rival, Montreal-based Bombardier. If Embraer had had Bombardier's employment cost structure, its operating margin would have fallen from 21% of revenues to 7%, and its net income would have turned negative. Unsurprisingly, Embraer has focused its operations on final assembly, which is the most labor-intensive part of the production process, and has outsourced other operating activities to its supplier partners.

Labor arbitrage can be applied to R&D as well as to ongoing operations, as Embraer also demonstrates. The company is currently preparing for the certification and initial delivery of a 70-seater, the first model in a new, larger family of regional jets. When it was announced in 1999, the plane was projected to cost $850 million to develop. It would have cost $100 million more, the company estimated, had the 10 million engineering man-hours involved in developing the new family come from Canada.

One might argue that labor arbitrage is an unsustainable strategy in knowledge industries because labor costs quickly rise to match demand. But the experience of East Asian economies suggests that even if one assumes labor costs will converge in the long run (or that costs will eventually reflect productivity levels), the period between now and then can extend into decades. Indeed, the top Indian software services firms have consistently posted returns on capital employed in the range of 50% to 75% and have grown at 30% to 40% a year over the past decade. And the prospects are for continued profitable growth, in part because the reduction in large companies' technology budgets makes labor cost advantages more important.

At first sight, capital cost differentials would seem to offer slimmer pickings than labor cost differences; they are measured in single percentage points rather than multiples of ten or 20. But considering that most companies (at least in the United States) earn returns within two to three percentage points of their cost of capital, such differences *are* consequential, especially in capital-intensive industries. Thus, Cemex, the international cement company headquartered in Mexico, has striven to reduce the effects of "Mexico risk" on its finances not just by listing the company on the New York Stock Exchange. More uniquely among Mexican companies, Cemex has also folded the ownership of all its non-Mexican assets into its operations in Spain (where interest costs are lower and are tax deductible) and has formed investment partnerships with entities such as the insurer AIG and the private equity arm of the Government of Singapore Investment Corporation. These moves have reportedly helped reduce Cemex's capital costs by several hundred basis points and has solidified its position as the world's most profitable international cement manufacturer (as well as the largest trader).

The subtlest forms of economic arbitrage involve the exploitation of knowledge differentials.[2] Forget, for a moment, the tangible aspects of Cemex's international operations and focus on its internationally recruited knowledge workers. The company seeks out graduates of leading business and other professional schools around the world and creates career paths for them that involve sending them abroad and immersing them in foreign cultures. (CEO Lorenzo Zambrano himself has an MBA from Stanford.) The company also makes heavy use of foreign (mostly U.S.) management and technical consultants and benchmarks its performance against best-in-class foreign companies (like Federal Express in logistics). Some analysts see these international influences as key ingredients in Cemex's heavy emphasis on information technology, as well as in its decision to remain focused on the cement industry and expand geographically rather than diversify into other industries—the model followed by most other Mexican conglomerates. Whatever the truth of the claim, there is no doubt that the diverse experiences of Cemex's international workforce has broadened the company's horizons.

Reconciling Difference and Similarity

One would think companies that try to exploit differences would not find it easy to exploit similarities as well. And indeed, a large body of research on the horizontal versus the vertical multinational enterprise has shown that there are fundamental tensions between pursuing scale economies and playing the spreads. (See the table "Conflicting Challenges.") The data indicate that there is some merit to classifying companies according to the primary way they add value through their international operations over long periods of time. But that either/or characterization of globalization strategies is very broad. Finer-grained analysis of case studies—particularly of companies that have in various ways been global innovators—suggests that it is possible to combine the two approaches to some extent. (See "A Brief History of Globalization and Arbitrage" at the end of this article.)

For a start, it's possible to apply different strategies to different elements of a business. Cemex pursued a financial strategy of arbitraging capital cost differences even as it implemented a standardized operational strategy. It set up complete, uniform production-to-distribution chains in most of its major markets, reinforced by cross-border scale economies in such areas as trading, logistics, information technology, and innovation (in the broadest sense of the term). Mixing and matching was possible in this case because, to a large extent, Cemex can choose how to raise capital independently from the way it chooses to compete in product markets.

Some companies have gone further. Consider the case of GE Medical Systems (GEMS), the division that Jeffrey Immelt built up between 1997 and 2000 before he was tapped to take over from Jack Welch as CEO. Immelt pushed for acquisitions to build up scale because, for the leading global competitors, an R&D-to-sales ratio of at least 8% represented a significant source of scale economies. But he also implemented a production strategy that was intended to arbitrage cost differences by concentrating manufacturing operations—and,

Conflicting Challenges

The challenges facing companies pursuing economies of scale through adaptation or aggregation are fundamentally different from those that companies face when pursuing absolute economies through arbitrage.

	Adaptation or Aggregation	Arbitrage
Competitive Advantage Why globalize at all?	To achieve scale and scope economies through standardization	To reap absolute economies through specialization
Configuration Why locate in foreign countries?	To minimize the effects of distance by concentrating on foreign countries that are similar to one's home base	To exploit distance by operating in a more diverse set of countries
Coordination How should international operations be organized?	By business; to achieve economies of scale across borders by placing a greater emphasis on horizontal relationships	By function; to achieve absolute economies by placing a greater emphasis on vertical relationships (efficiently matching supply and demand across borders, for instance)
Control Systems What are the strategic dangers?	Excessive standardization, on the one hand; variety, complexity, or both, on the other	Narrowing differences between countries
Corporate Diplomacy What public issues need to be addressed?	The appearance of, and backlash against, cultural or other forms of domination (especially by U.S. companies)	The exploitation or bypassing of suppliers, channels, or intermediaries

ultimately, other activities—wherever in the world they could be carried out most cost effectively. By 2001, GEMS obtained 15% of its direct material purchases from, and had located 40% of its own manufacturing activities in, low-cost countries.

Like Cemex, GEMS was able to pursue both approaches because it could organize its operations into relatively autonomous bundles of activities (like product development) in which economies of scale and standardization were essential and those (like procurement and manufacturing) where arbitrage economies were being pursued. What's more, it was able to coordinate its widely dispersed operations by applying centrally developed learning templates. In particular, Immelt applied the "pitcher-catcher concept," developed elsewhere in GE, in which for each move, a pitching team at a high-cost existing plant works with a catching team at a low-cost new location, and the move is not considered complete until the performance of the catching team meets or exceeds that of the pitching team. As a result, GEMS (and GE) seems to have managed to move production to low-cost countries faster than European competitors such as Philips and Siemens while also benefiting from greater scale economies.

But even the best management can get only so far in melding the two strategies. Acer, one of the world's largest computer manufacturers, supplies a cautionary tale of what can happen when companies go too far. Acer entered early into the contract manufacturing of personal computers, operating in low-wage Taiwan, and made good money with that arbitrage play. But in the early 1990s, it began to push Acer as a global brand, particularly in developed markets. This two-track approach turned out to be problematic. The branded business

grew to significant volumes but continued to generate
losses because the competitive environment was particularly tough for a late mover. Meanwhile, customers for
Acer's contract-manufacturing arm worried that their
business secrets would spill over to its competing line
of business. They also feared that Acer could cross-
subsidize its own brand with profits from its contract-
manufacturing operations and so undercut their prices.
In 2000, the strategy blew up when IBM canceled a
major order, reducing its share of Acer's total contract-
manufacturing revenues from 53% in the first quarter of
2000 to only 26% in the second quarter of 2001.

Acer responded by making some hard choices. Contract manufacturing has remained focused on customers
in developed countries—and will gradually be spun off
into a separate company. Meanwhile, sales of its own
branded products have been focused on the East Asia
region, particularly Greater China, where the contract
customers cannot sell at a low enough price to compete.
With this move, the company has acknowledged that the
logic of exploiting similarities often calls for targeting
countries similar to a company's home base, whereas the
logic of arbitrage involves exploiting one or more of the
differences inherent in distance.

The future of the globalization process is by no means
obvious. Markets may integrate further once economic
conditions improve. But some argue that the process
could actually shift into reverse, toward even greater economic isolation, if the experience between the two World
Wars is any precedent. Whatever the ultimate direction,
though, the differences that make arbitrage valuable as
well as the similarities that create scale economies will
remain with us for the foreseeable future. That spells

opportunity for those companies that have the imagination to see the full range of possibilities.

Complex Aggregation Strategies

A NUMBER OF STRATEGISTS HAVE proposed that rather than adapt its business model country by country, a company should organize its operating units along regional lines, business lines, or some combination of both. The idea is to avoid thinking in terms of a country-level trade-off between localization and standardization and instead build global networks that can share knowledge, find and train global managers, and create a truly global corporate culture.

The most famous practitioner of this approach was ABB's Percy Barnevik, who broke up the bureaucracy and geographic fiefdoms he had inherited in the power and automation-technology company created by the merger of Asea of Sweden and Brown, Boveri of Switzerland. He flattened the organization and fragmented its businesses into small, local operating companies that reported to both a country manager and a business-area manager—a matrix, or dual basis of aggregation. This approach helped ABB digest acquisitions and reorganize and refocus operating units on new opportunities. The business-country matrix itself wasn't new, but ABB was one of the few companies that seemed to be able to make it work, through groundbreaking management information systems and many other linking mechanisms, both formal and informal.

Yet, as ABB was to demonstrate, complex aggregation schemes are hugely expensive and hard to manage. The challenge is magnified by the fact that there aren't just two potential dimensions for aggregation, countries and product lines, but many others as well: function, competence, client industry, key accounts, and on and on. Indeed, in 1993, Barnevik himself added a regional overlay to the matrix by grouping countries into three regions. Five years later, his successor as CEO, Göran Lindahl, removed this overlay because it was too costly.

Under Lindahl, ABB moved toward a more traditional global structure, organized by products, and also developed a global account-management structure to serve key accounts across borders. But pressures on the company continued to mount as a result of a slowdown in demand in the wake of the Asian financial crisis, which caused prices to plunge and efficiency requirements to escalate. These conditions complicated ABB's already intricate efforts to market systems that integrated products from different business areas or for which the key customers were global or regional, not local. There were also other problems intertwined with the autonomy of the local companies.

In 2001, new CEO Jörgen Centerman replaced the matrix with a structure that combined front-end operations in a different way than it grouped its back-end functions. Specifically, ABB created four main customer-oriented units, defined by the industries (rather than the countries) that the customers were in, which were supposed to enhance the company's ability to create value for its global and regional customers in particular. Then it also created two back-end technological units, Power Technologies and Automation Technologies, which (assuming that appropriate linking mechanisms could be created) were supposed to aggregate technology development across the businesses in each of ABB's two main areas of technological competence.

Centerman, however, was forced out in 2002, amid pressures associated with the sluggishness of this new organization and asbestos-related liabilities picked up in the acquisition (under Barnevik) of the U.S. company Combustion Engineering. His successor, Jürgen Dormann, dismantled the front-end/back-end organization, which was deemed unworkable, sold off portions of the front end, and regrouped the remaining businesses into two divisions—Power Systems and Automation—thereby returning the company to just one primary basis of aggregation, products. But losses grew from $691 million in 2001 to $787 million in 2002, and questions persisted in mid-2003 about whether a turnaround was really at hand.

Perhaps the broader moral from the ABB story is that attempting to organize a global business without first understanding what one is hoping to achieve through cross-border activities—in particular whether one is trying to exploit similarities or differences—is a bit like putting the proverbial cart before the horse. Indeed, to limit the strategic discussion to structure and process is to presuppose that there is only one best global strategy. The discussion in this article should convince you that this is not the case.

A Brief History of Globalization and Arbitrage

PROBABLY THE SINGLE MOST overlooked fact in the history of globalization and strategy is that, for a number of centuries, firms' international economic activities were motivated entirely by considerations of arbitrage. The great trading companies of the seventeenth and eighteenth centuries arbitraged across extreme differences in cost and availability created by geography. Spices, to take just one example, could be grown in the East Indies but not in Northern Europe, where they originally cost several hundred times as much.

Arbitrage was also the strategy of the global whaling fleets of the late eighteenth century (which, with their floating factory ships, can be said to have originated offshore manufacturing). It was also behind the vertically integrated agricultural and mining companies that arose relatively early in the nineteenth century. The freestanding enterprises that dominated British foreign direct investment through the latter part of the nineteenth century attempted to arbitrage across differences in administrative structure (and power) by pursuing foreign investment opportunities under British law. Exports of labor-intensive, capital-light manufactured goods—textiles and clothing, for instance—by countries with relatively low labor costs involved arbitrage as well, but of economic rather than geographic or administrative differences.

The pursuit of scale, rather than of absolute, economies is quite new. Replicating successful business models in new locations didn't begin until the end of the nineteenth century. Since then, however, it has become the dominant strategy, which is why the *net* effect of most types of distance between countries is to reduce the economic activity between them.

Notes

1. For an even more extensive, market-based review of the evidence, see my article, "Semiglobalization and Interna-

tional Business Strategy," *Journal of International Business Studies*, June 2003.

2. Arbitrage aficionados are also fond of talking about "dynamic arbitrage," in which a broader global presence can enable companies to exploit exchange rate changes and other volatile financial fluctuations more quickly and efficiently. But the general benefits from such efforts, beyond pure portfolio insurance effects, remain in doubt.

Originally published in November 2003
Reprint R0311E

About the Contributors

PANKAJ GHEMAWAT is the Jaime and Josefina Chua Tiampo Professor of Business Administration at the Harvard Business School in Boston.

JOHN L. GRAHAM is a professor of international business at the Graduate School of Management at the University of California, Irvine.

N. MARK LAM is an attorney and business adviser specializing in East-West negotiations.

GEOFFREY LIEBERTHAL is a consultant with Bain & Company in San Francisco.

KENNETH LIEBERTHAL is the William Davidson Professor of Corporate Strategy and International Business, the China Director of the Davidson Institute, and a professor of political science at the University of Michigan in Ann Arbor. He is also a Senior Director of Stonebridge International, a Washington, D.C.–based global business consulting firm.

VLADIMIR PUCIK is a professor of international human resources and strategy at the International Institute for Management Development (IMD) in Lausanne, Switzerland.

WILFRIED VANHONACKER, a professor of marketing and a Senior Wei Lun Fellow at Hong Kong University of Science and Technology, is a former Dean of China Europe International Business School in Shanghai.

PETER J. WILLIAMSON is an affiliate professor of Asian business and international management at Insead.

KATHERINE XIN is a professor of management and holds the Michelin Chair in Leadership and Human Resource Management at China Europe International Business School in Shanghai; she is also the Editor in Chief of HBR China.

RICK YAN is a Vice President in the Beijing office of Bain & Company, where he specializes in multinational companies in China.

MING ZENG is an assistant professor of Asian business at Insead in Singapore and a visiting professor at the Cheung Kong Graduate School of Business in Beijing.

Index